THE
BOOK
OF
SPELLS

previously published as *The Teen Spell Book*

THE
BOOK
OF
SPELLS

The Magick of Witchcraft

Jamie Della

TEN SPEED PRESS
California | New York

Contents

Introduction 1

THE
PATH

THE
CRAFT

THE
SPELLS

Emotional, Spiritual, and Physical Health

Knowledge and Self-Knowledge

SPELL—To cast your word upon the world

MAGICK—The relationship between focused will and Universal energy

WITCHCRAFT—An ethical and empathic path of shaping the unseen forces

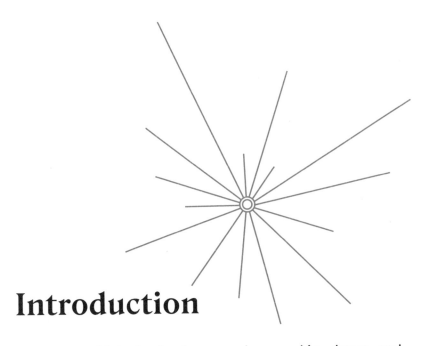

Introduction

As a young girl, I relentlessly pursued every whim, dream, and desire that crossed the movie screen of my mind. I knew no fear. I believed in angels and guides from the world of Spirit, also known as the Great Mystery, Universe, God, Goddess, or any name you prefer. The idea of *Spirit* may be new to some people, and so I want to emphasize that each time I reference Spirit, I am pointing to an energetic force of Love and Light that is known by many names. I have chosen the name Spirit because it resonates with me and it is most often used to identify this Divine power. Spirit guides can be deities, angels, animals, crystals, ancestors, plants, directions, elements, or any other beneficial energy or entity.

I have always been aware of the subtle energies around me, from a passing stranger's sidelong glance to the cool tingle that indicates the presence of Spirit. In time, I excitedly tried to share my experiences with others. I wasn't well received. It was as if I were speaking a different language when I spoke of miracles or the profound impact of Spirit on my life. People called me weird and shut me out. Feeling hurt and alone, I worked hard to quiet the opinions, comments, and judgments of others so I could listen to the inner voice of my own free will, knowing, and individual spark.

At first, I was reckless and chased every wild whim (some quite dangerous) just to prove that I was in control of my decisions, but true self-reliance needs no approval from others. Instead of following the angry voice screaming at me to rebel against society and break down all my boundaries, I began to listen to the quieter, calming one within.

I am not saying we shouldn't push our limitations once in a while. That youthful teenage impulse to challenge everything is what keeps society from conforming to one mindset and us from falling dormant in a mundane, colorless life. I still took risks, but the risks I'm talking about pertain to a willingness to be who I was meant to be—a beloved and proud child of Spirit. This unbreakable, unapologetic will to be true to yourself is the cornerstone of magick.

Before I wrote the previous edition of this book, *The Teen Spell Book*, in 2001, I knew I was still angry and hurt about things that had happened in my past and I was letting these bitter feelings affect my present. It can be a long journey to heal wounds from our youth and teen years, especially if you bury them deep inside. I knew writing *The Teen Spell Book* would bring up these hurt feelings, but I also understood these wounds had become underlying negative influences in my life. It was a daring adventure! I read through old diaries from my teen years and sought out all the times I had felt disconnected from Spirit and my own lovability. I associated an emotion or action with each of these moments and wrote meditations, visualizations, and affirmations—that is, spells—to move toward my divinity and unconditional self-love.

In *The Book of Spells,* I hope to once again reach out, help you up, and serve as a nonjudgmental and accepting presence while you embark on your unique path of expression and connection with Spirit. It is difficult to be a lone light in a world where most others find it easier to shroud themselves in darkness—but do not give up. You are not alone.

Sisters and brothers, we are torchbearers emerging from darkness, bringing the light of awareness to the forefront of society. "We cannot solve our problems with the same thinking we used when we created them," said Albert Einstein. You possess the talent and ability to make all your dreams come true. The honor of keeping the lore of these wise ancient teachings alive rests on your capable shoulders. You have the power. You *are* power. You are the medicine you have been looking for.

"Be it remembered that when the fault is found the remedy lies not in a battle against this and not in a use of willpower and energy to suppress a wrong, but in a steady development of the opposite virtue, thus automatically washing from our natures all trace of the offender. To forget the failing and consciously strive to develop the virtue which would make the former impossible, this is true victory."
—Dr. Edward Bach, founder of Bach Flower Remedies

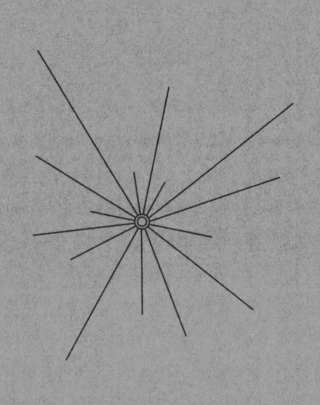

THE
PATH

Following the Path

It is a personal choice whether you identify as a Witch or a Wiccan. Wicca is an earth-based lifestyle and hierarchical religion. Being a Witch is also an earth-based lifestyle, but self-directed. Both paths follow and celebrate the rhythm of nature and abide by the Wiccan Rede, "Do what thou will as long as you harm none" (often shortened to simply "Harm None") and the Threefold Law, "Whatever you do comes back to you three times three times three." Both paths celebrate meaningful traditions that reach deep into ancient matriarchal societies.

Earth-based religions predate Christianity, Judaism, Buddhism, and Hinduism. Relics, cave drawings, and other evidence of nature worship date back more than thirty-five thousand years. Ancient followers honored the two forces: the female Goddess of fertility, creation, and the birth giver the male God of the hunt, death and rebirth, and the essence of the fields and forests.

Spirit is a balance of these two energies. These followers celebrated the natural forces, cycles of the seasons, and life with ritual, song, and personal attunement with Spirit.

It was not until the early to mid 1900s that brave souls such as Isaac Bonewits, Gerald Gardner, Charles Godfrey Leland, Margaret Murray, Doreen Valiente, Patricia Crowther, Stewart Farrar, and Raymond Buckland came out of the broom closet to openly speak about the Wiccan religion and its teachings. Writings from a selection of these figures and those of the next generation such as Scott Cunningham, Margot Adler, Raven Grimassi, Z. Budapest, and Starhawk are noted in Recommended Reading (page 209).

TRADITIONS

There are many traditions and ways of practicing the Path, whether you call yourself a Witch or a Wiccan. Although the approach to attain spiritual connection with the Divine will differ within these traditions, you must always maintain your integrity to "Harm None" and the awareness that whatever energy you send out will be returned to you threefold.

I suggest you research all avenues available to you before choosing your Path. Take the time to see if you are a good fit for the tradition, the coven, and the people in the coven (since some groups will not admit someone who is not unanimously approved by all the members). Some covens host open gatherings for non-initiates to enjoy the experiences and learn more. Find out if there are open circles festivals, or conferences in your community and take advantage of any opportunities to learn more about the different traditions. You might also decide to study magick without choosing a pantheon to follow!

Instead, begin by familiarizing yourself with the Goddesses and Gods throughout time and across the globe listed on pages 22–37. You can and will develop your own style of what magick means to you.

Modern Witchcraft is a culmination of ancient wisdoms and teachings to meet the needs and desires of today's Spirit is constantly being revealed to the blessed children of the Universe in new ways. We are each a ray of light from the great source of all that is. There is no need for a mediator between you and Spirit. You are the Goddess. You are the God. You are a Divine Being.

Gardnerian

Gerald Gardner joined an English coven of Witches in the 1930s and subsequently brought Wicca to the public in the 1950s. He was the first to publicly speak about the Craft, and we owe much of its survival to his courage. Wicca is an oathbound mystery tradition, and so there are limits to what non-initiates can know. This is largely to preserve the mysteries until they are revealed in the initiation or elevations. The Gardnerian tradition includes a degree system of advancement where no self-initiation is allowed. Covens perform magick in a circle and work *skyclad* (naked) in order to obscure social distinctions based on attire. Some feel nakedness brings you closer to nature and that clothing restricts bodily movement in the raising of magickal power. Gardnerians scourge to purify themselves before rituals and to release unwanted energy. Some covens strive to have an equal number of females and males during ceremony; this is known as a "perfect couple" and is a simulation of the perfect union of Goddess and God.

In their effort to attune themselves to nature, followers honor the God of animals, hunting, death and rebirth, as well as the Goddess of vegetation, the moon, and the earth, who is also known as the Great Mother. Followers emphasize the role of the Goddess in lunar rituals and worship, whereas the God's role is more important in seasonal rituals. There is debate about whether Gardner's tradition is just an unchanged version of an ancient religion, but no matter the case, he was sincere in celebrating a happy, peaceful, nature-loving way of worship. The Farrars, key figures in the Wiccan community, teach the beliefs and workings of a similar tradition, descended from Gardnerian Wicca. Vivianne Crowley's *Wicca: The Old Religion in the New Age* is a recommended book for further study.

Alexandrian

Founded by Alex and Maxine Sanders, this tradition has rituals that are similar to those of the Gardnerian tradition. They work with the same Book of Shadows and same Gods and Goddesses. The main difference between these two paths of Witchcraft is in their philosophical approach. Alexandrian Witches focus on training personal freedom, beauty, and the power that comes from that freedom. The Witch gets more individual choice and is less secretive in their magickal practice. In addition, the Alexandrian path emphasizes further occult development with some strong leanings toward the Kabbalah. Reference Brian Cain's works for additional information on the Alexandrian tradition.

Dianic

The Dianic tradition was popularized by Ann Forfreedom, Ruth Barrett, Z. Budapest, and focuses on feminist and humanist issues and concerns. Followers honor the Goddess Diana, encourage female leadership and matriarchal traditions, and celebrate mythos. Although members are most often strictly female, male participants are welcomed in some covens. There is a strong emphasis on the Goddess and her three aspects as Maiden, Mother, and Crone.

In the Dianic tradition, the Goddess of Ten Thousand Names and female-bodied individuals are celebrated. The Goddess requires no God and woman requires no man. The female is considered primary: whole and complete unto herself, without any type of binary needed to create life, magic, or transformation. The Dianic tradition is very popular among lesbians and female-identifying persons who prefer to worship, if not live entirely, free of males. In fact, one of the key points in this tradition is faith in the possibility of parthenogenesis, where the female body creates life without male intervention. Other Dianic core values include the privacy of the Goddess, the beautiful mysteries of the female body, kinship with nature, working with tree Spirits and Spirits of place, and a sensitivity to the pulse and rhythm of the Universe. By accepting the human revolution around the axis that is the Goddess, followers strive to live revolutionary ideals and study the forbidden or forgotten histories of women and Goddesses. Z. Budapest's books offer in-depth insight into this tradition (see Recommended Reading, page 209).

Italian

Italian Witchcraft is also known as Stregheria, the Old Religion, La Vecchia Religone, or simply La Vecchia (The Old Ways). According to legend, this religion was taught by Aradia, daughter of the Goddess Diana, the Queen of the Witches. This reportedly began in the four-teenth century and spread through the creation of three systems known as the Fanarra (earth and forest mysteries), Janarra (moon mysteries), and Tanarra (stellar mysteries).

Followers believe in Lares, a group of Spirits that provide a connection with one's ancestral family lineage. A core tenet of Italian Witchcraft is that the "one creator" is both feminine and masculine. This Divine Being exists in all of creation.

Other beliefs include reincarnation, karma, and psychic abilities. Aradia also taught her disciples that they have powerful gifts, which include the ability to bring success in love, call forth Spirits, hear the voice of the wind in nature, divine the future, and reveal hidden things.

For further information on Italian Witchcraft, please read Raven Grimassi's *The Italian Witchcraft, Book of the Holy Strega,* and *Heredity Witchcraft* and visit Stregheria.com.

Celtic

The Celtic tradition is an ancient practice that originated in Scotland and Ireland. Its popularization is not attributed to one teacher. This sect focuses on solar and lunar changes, the balance and harmony between the God and Goddess, and attunement with nature. Followers practice meditation, divination, and magickal herbalism. It emphasizes the Celtic pantheon, history, traditions, food, and music. Solitary practitioners may find this tradition easy to follow since it does not require initiation.

Tree lore is very important within this tradition. The revered and sacred trees are oak, ash, apple, hazel, alder, elder, and yew. Followers honor deities associated with sacred wells and other healing places. Power from the land itself is huge in Celtic spirituality, as well as a deep faith in faeries and otherworldly beings such as ghosts and mythical beasts. The faeries, sometimes called the *fae*, are so small that they are regarded as "the Little People," while others such as the Tuatha de Danann, also known as "the Shining Ones," are quite large. Read Edain McCoy's books for information on the Celtic practice of Witchcraft (see Recommended Reading, page 209).

Faerie

Founded by Victor Anderson and Gwydion Pendderwen, the Faerie tradition focuses on nature and ecological issues and concerns. Followers revere the one creator and acknowledge this Divine light within every being. They also honor animal Spirits and the power and protection they provide. The Faerie tradition supports the idea that life exists in a symbolic, transitory, and harmonizing spiral dance of constantly moving energy; nothing ever stays the same. This is similar to the Buddhist theory that all mental states and material objects are impermanent.

The Faerie tradition emphasizes Mother Earth's energy and her angelic protectors of nature, known as faeries. The word *faerie* is said to have its roots in the Gaelic word *sith* or *sidhe,* which has several meanings: hill or mound, Divine, unearthly, supernatural, and peace. Faerie is also said to have derived from the Latin word *fatum,* or "fate", which refers to the Goddesses who control and rule over human destiny; *fatare,* which means "to enchant or mystify"; and *fatuae,* which translates to "a race of immortal feminine beings." Faeries are most powerful during the in-between times such as twilight and the moment just before waking up from sleep. Kisma Stepanich's books provide additional information about the Faerie tradition.

Norse

The Norse tradition (also known as Heathenry) is a reconstructed path from ancient sources that includes magickal, practical, and social practices. You do not have to be initiated nor of a certain heritage to follow the Heathen practice. Modern rituals are typically performed clothed, often in Viking-era garb. Followers weave honor and mythology from Norse and Icelandic resources (known as "the Lore"), ancient customs, languages, and pantheon into their magickal practice.

The two main tribes of Gods in the Heathen pantheon are the Aesir and the Vanir. The Aesir include the widely known Gods and Goddesses Odin (or Old Saxon Wodan), Frigg, and Thor, and the tribe is associated mostly with war and thought. The Vanir are associated with wisdom, fertility, the sea, agriculture, and being able to see the future. They include the well-known Freyr, Freya, and Njord.

The runes, a divination system inhabiting the ancient alphabet of the Elder Futhark, is an important part of Heathen practice today. According to the *Hávamál* (stanzas 139–46), the mysteries of the runes were revealed to Odin when he hung himself from the World Tree (Yggdrasil) for nine days and nights. Author Diana Paxson is an excellent resource for books on Norse traditions in magick. To learn more about runes, see page 50.

Egyptian

The wise Egyptian teachings have existed for centuries. Followers of the Egyptian path stress the importance of infusing magick in amulets, scripts, spells, names, and rituals. Ancient Egyptian beliefs are based on a polytheistic approach consisting of the original creators, the Ogduat, and the Gods and Goddess that spun off of from those. They believe that each human being is a compilation of nine bodies that make the whole of a person's existence. After a person dies, they must address the Goddess Ma'at with the forty-two Negative Confessions, which are a lot like the Ten Commandments. The soul must confess to not committing these acts before Ma'at, who will then weigh that person's heart against her feather. Anubis passes judgment over the heart and Mafdet carries out the sentence. The heart, not the mind, is the seat of the soul to Ancient Egyptians and those who practice its magick.

The Egyptian tradition rests upon the reverence for the rise of the star Sothis, which ancient Egyptians believed dictated the inundation of the Nile River. These floods distributed the fertile silt needed to grow abundant crops and sealed the fate of the rulers' ability to be prosperous for their people. Eleanor L. Harris wrote excellent books on ancient Egyptian Magick (See Recommended Reading, page 209).

SABBATS

Earth-based spirituality means followers live in tune with the ever-changing essence of nature. Witches and Wiccans follow the cycles of the moon and the seasons and live in accordance with the natural rhythm of life. Our church is Mother Nature, whether we worship in a field, a forest, the mountains, the desert, or on a beach. There are eight nature-based holidays (holy days) known as sabbats. Each sabbat connects us to nature by celebrating the ever-changing earth—so much like ourselves. These holidays, spaced six weeks apart, embrace special, sacred points on the Great Solar Wheel of the Year, also known as the Mandala of Nature. When you cast spells, try to match your pure intention with the nature of the season. Your spells will be stronger and work better if you do.

Samhain

The first sabbat is Samhain, also known as Halloween, the third and final harvest and the Witches' New Year, and is celebrated on October 31. During this holiday, decorate your altar with pomegranates, apples, pumpkins, gourds, pictures of deceased loved ones, autumn leaves, or marigold plants. *Samhain* means "summer's end." It is the time of year that the veil between the two worlds—that of the living and dead, human and faerie, and other parallel universes—is considered to be the thinnest. Samhain is the time we trade information with people who have died and other spiritual beings as we give thanks for our ancestors. Death is recognized as part of the natural cycle of birth and rebirth. As the opposite side of death is birth, this holiday is the time for new beginnings and hopes for manifesting of our dreams for the new year.

Winter Solstice

Winter Solstice, or Yule, is the longest night of the year, falling between December 20 and 22. Possible altar decorations include evergreens, pinecones, wreaths, mistletoe, holly, candles, berries, or images of the sun. Some women stay up all night the night before the Winter Solstice to help Mother Earth get through the labor and birth of the sun. The darkness, the womb, is where all creation originates. It is a time of quiet reflection; if we pay attention to the voice inside, we can think clearly and amazing ideas can be born. At Yule we celebrate the sun's growing strength. *Solstice* means "sun stand still," while *Yule* translates as "wheel." The wheel is symbolic of the Wheel of the Year, the ever-changing, never-ending cycle of birth, death, and rebirth.

Candlemas

Candlemas, also known as Brigid's Day or Imbolc falls, on February 1 or 2. Options for decorating your altar include candles, incense, seeds, nuts, vessels containing water, or herbal teas. This is the time of year when, in the dark of a winter's night, the first seeds of light and inspiration are planted. This holiday is a perfect example of the Threefold Law ("Whatever you do comes back to you three times three times three"). You hold the paintbrushes to the canvas of your life. Whatever you sow, you reap; whatever you put out in the Universe comes back to you. Brigid, the Goddess of fire, inspiration, and water wells, rules this holiday.

Spring Equinox

On the Spring Equinox, or Ostara, which falls between March 20 and 22, night and day last equally as long. Decorate your altar with representations of spring and new life (such as rabbits, birds, baby animals, or flowers) or images of fertility (such as eggs, nuts, or seeds). Spring has begun, and with it, a celebration of rebirth and growth. Seeds planted in the darkness of winter are beginning to sprout and flower. Spring Equinox is a time to honor the darkness and the light, life and death; to explore the balance in our lives and nature; to give expression to our impish, playful behavior; and to cast spells for balance, harmony, and equality. This festival pays respect to Ostara, the German Goddess of rebirth, dawn, and growth. She is also known as Ēostre, from which we get the name for Easter, falling on the Sunday after the Spring Equinox full moon. All things green, fertility, and abundance are honored on this holiday.

Beltane

Beltane, also known as May Day, celebrates the pure joy of being alive and rejoices in all of nature's creations. Decorate your altar with flowers, images of faeries, creamy treats for faeries, pictures of you truly enjoying yourself, maypoles, ribbons, or oak leaves and branches. It is the great spring festival of the Goddess. Gardens are beginning to grow, hibernating animals are waking, and all forms of creativity are celebrated. Beltane is also the holiday of fertility. On April 30, celebrants light huge bonfires and literally party all night. The next day they erect a maypole (symbolic of the God) and wind ribbons (representative of the Goddess) around the pole. The result represents the child. As fertility is a power—the power of creation—we must have respect for its strength and the results it brings. It must come at a time when we are mature enough to handle the outcome.

Summer Solstice

Summer Solstice, also known as Midsummer, is the best time to harvest herbs and pick flowers for healing purposes. You can decorate your altar with flowers (especially roses), herbs, and pictures or other representations of the sun, such as a sunflower. Add anything to your altar that you are ready to give up. On June 20 through 22, the sun is at its strongest, and whichever day this holiday falls on will be the longest of the year. Since this is a fire festival, all things round, orange, or yellow are celebrated as a representation of the life-giving sun, an aspect of the God. After the Summer Solstice, the sun will begin to wane and fade in power. It is a reminder that life is not static; nothing lasts forever. Life, people, places, and things are always changing. Midsummer is the time to celebrate the joys life has brought you and practice letting go of things that no longer serve your highest good. Cast spells for self-empowerment during this holiday.

Lammas

Lammas, or Lughnasadh, is celebrated on August 1 or 2. Possible altar decorations include breads, corn, berries, grains, harvested fruits and vegetables, or pictures and symbols of all your hopes and fears for the coming year. The Wheel of the Year has turned to the first harvest. We reap the rewards of our hard work as we harvest corn and wheat. Because of the wheat harvest, this holiday is also known as the Festival of Breads. We are the guardians of all the seeds we have planted. On Lammas we begin the quiet season of facing our hopes and fears, as well as getting to know the unseen and hidden sides of ourselves. Although the days are probably still warm, winter—also known as the "dark season"—is approaching, and so much can happen. It is time to make friends with our shadow selves, the part of our beings that points to where we need the most love, pure expression, improvement, or the light and space to shine.

Autumnal Equinox

The Autumnal or Fall Equinox, also known as Mabon, is the other day of the year (along with the Spring Equinox) when night and day are in balance. You can choose to decorate your altar with garlands of greenery and apples, harvested dried corn, winter squash, pomegranates, pumpkins, autumn leaves, nuts, or seeds. It is another season to cast spells for balance and harmony and to honor the cycle of birth, death, and rebirth as we begin the dark season of the Goddess. The warmth of the sun is fading, and the nights are getting longer. The Autumnal Equinox is the time for introspection and self-evaluation. This holiday marks the second harvest. As we gather the vegetables, fruits, nuts, and grain that are ripe, we give thanks. The Autumnal Equinox is the Wiccan or Witches Thanksgiving. We celebrate the coming of fall on September 20 through 22.

DEITIES

Along with casting particular spells during certain seasons, your spells will also be more potent if you call on the guardianship, protection, and wisdom of that aspect of the Goddess or God that rules during that season. When we cast spells and ask the protection or guidance of a particular deity, we call for that aspect of the Divine source to help our dreams come true. For example, if you wanted love in your life, you might ask Aphrodite or Venus to help. If you needed protection, you could call on Hecate or Thor. When calling upon more than one deity, it is suggested that you select from within the same culture. Some cultures are similar and their deities will work well together, but other pairings could be marred by historical conflicts, such as colonization and genocide, or specific traditions that each need to be acknowledged when casting a spell.

I have placed a ★ by the deities that one should know on an intimate level for at least one year before asking for their help. You can study their culture, dedicate an altar, and seek guidance from someone who has worked with the deity. The spells found in this book feature deities I am familiar with and personally call upon often; make your selection as is fitting for you.

All deities have symbols associated with their magick, such as Athena's owl and olive branch, which you can include in your spellwork or incorporate on your altar. Sometimes the deity will seem familiar, as if you have dedicated an altar to them in a previous lifetime or they are coded in your DNA. I have listed some common associations for each deity, but you will find that each God and Goddess has a unique, ancient, and deep lore that requires commitment and a strong connection to fully understand. For example, the Hunt is associated with Cernunnos and Diana, but this encompasses more than just hunting deer or elk; it also refers to the Hunt for the Holy Grail and the search for the Divinity within. The qualities listed in this section and throughout the spells in this book will give you an introductory understanding of Gods and Goddesses. If interested in learning more, refer to Recommended Reading (page 209) for resources to help you on your journey to forging a connection with your chosen deity. As you cultivate your intention and invest time and dedication into this working relationship, you will find the deity's qualities growing stronger in you.

You will notice that deities associated with the same sabbats carry similar characteristics that are in harmony with the season. For instance, during the Spring Equinox, many of the Gods and Goddesses are related to vegetation or fertility. The deities' symbols and attributes are also linked to the male and female associations with the season. I begin with Samhain because it is considered the Witches' and Wiccan New Year.

Samhain Goddesses and Associations

Al-llat *(Persian)*
Moon magick, the Underworld

Baba Yaga *(Russian)*
The Crone

Bast *(Egyptian)*
Cats, joy, music, dancing,
healing, moon, fertility

Cerridwen *(Welsh-Scottish)*
Wisdom, inspiration, new
endeavors, shape-shifting,
knowledge, magick

Epona/Rhiannon
(Celtic-Gaulish)
Mother, horse, abundance,
change, moon, fertility,
health, healing

Fortuna *(Greco-Roman)*
Fate, luck (both good and
bad), success

Frigg/Freya *(Norse)*
Love, sexuality, war,
protection, peace

Hecate *(Greek)*
Moon magick, divination, the
Underworld, justice, Witches,
dreams, knowledge,
protection, success

Hel *(Norse)*
Mystery, the Underworld

Inanna *(Sumerian)*
Earth, love, weaving, battle,
astrology, moon, rain, winged
lions, prophecy, "Queen
of Heaven"

Ishtar *(Babylonian)*
Earth, fertility, love, battle,
storms, marriage, divination

Kali *(Indian)*
Mother, destruction and death
necessary for rebirth, justice,
power, protection for women
against violence

Lilith *(Hebraic)*
Independence, obstacles

Mafdet *(Egyptian)*
Justice, cats, protection

Mari *(Basque)*
Moon magick, fire, earth,
Witches' protector, protection
from lies, theft, pride, and
arrogance

The Morrigan *(Celtic)*
Water and its healing
power, justice

Zorya Vechernaya *(Slavic)*
Sun, Triple Goddess,
well-being, protection

Samhain Gods and Associations

Am-Heh *(Egyptian)*
The Underworld, devourer, rebirth

Anubis *(Egyptian)*
Death, health, wisdom,
finder of lost things,
protection, communication

Corn Father *
(Native American)
Rebirth

Coyote Brother *
(Native American)
Trickster, humor, nature

Ghede * *(Vodun)*
Death, resurrection, protector
of children, healer

Hades *(Greek)*
The Underworld, elimination
of fear

Loki *(Norse)*
Trickster, cunning

Nefertum *(Egyptian)*
Setting sun, lotus, shedding
of old patterns or thoughts

Odin *(Norse)*
Father, war, magick, poetry,
cunning, the dead, creativity,
divination

Pluto *(Greco-Roman)*
The Underworld, fortune,
judgment, fire

Wodan *(Teutonic)*
Father, war, magick, poetry,
cunning, the dead

Winter Solstice Goddesses and Associations

Changing Woman * *(Apache)*
Shape-shifting

Eve *(Hebraic)*
New life, creation, fertility

Gaia *(Greek)*
Earth, love, fertility, heartbreak, marriage, divination, business

Heket *(Egyptian)*
Childbirth, resurrection, frog

Kuan Yin *(Chinese)*
Compassion, mercy, divination, magick, health, healing, protector of mothers and sailors; depicted with a lotus

Lilith *(Hebraic)*
Independence, obstacles

Ma'at *(Egyptian)*
Justice, truth, law, Divine order of the Universe, reincarnation

Metzli * *(Aztec)*
Moon, night, agriculture

Nox *(Roman)*
Night

Pandora *(Greek)*
Truth, hope, gifts

Pax *(Roman)*
Peace, harmony

Virgin Mary *(Christian)*
Creation, purity

Yemana * *(Yoruban)*
Mother Ocean, Holy Queen Sea, protection

Winter Solstice Gods and Associations

Aker *(Egyptian)*
Earth, ability to see in both directions, the Underworld

Apollo *(Greco-Roman)*
Sun, strength, courage, creativity, health, healing, justice, knowledge, intuition, success, heartbreak

Cronos *(Greek)*
Doorways, possibilities, new endeavors, turn of the year

Father Sun *(Native American)*
Sun

Helios *(Greek)*
Sun, riches, enlightenment

Horus *(Egyptian)*
Rebirth, sun, moon, prophecy, success, problem solving

Janus *(Roman)*
Doorways, possibilities, January, new endeavors, turn of the year, overcoming of obstacles, opportunity

Jesus *(Christian)*
Sun, rebirth

Llew/Lugh *(Welsh-Irish)*
Sun, war, skill, art, smithcrafting, knowledge, "of the long arm" or "of many arts"

Oak/Holly King *(Anglo-Celtic)*
Expansion and growth, restoration and withdrawal

Ra *(Egyptian)*
Father, sun, light

Saturn *(Roman)*
Faith, solitude, self-discipline, self-respect

Ukko *(Finnish-Slavic)*
Sky, air, thunder

Yachimata-Hiko *(Japanese)*
Possibilities, "innumerable roads"

Candlemas Goddesses and Associations

Anu *(Irish)*
Mother, abundance

Arachne *(Greek)*
Spider, weaving, destiny

Aradia *(Italian Streghe)*
Teacher, Witch Goddess

Arianrhod *(Welsh)*
Mother, reincarnation, stellar
movement

Athena *(Greek)*
Wisdom; courage; war;
protectress of architects,
weavers, sculptors, smithcrafters;
justice, creativity, business

Brigid *(Irish)*
Fire, wells, inspiration,
communication, poetry,
creativity, smithcrafting,
health, healing, new endeavors,
opportunity

Februa *(Roman)*
Cleansing, February

Gaia *(Greek)*
Earth, love, fertility, business,
heartbreak, marriage, divination

Inanna *(Sumerian)*
Earth, love, weaving, battle,
astrology, moon, rain, winged
lions, prophecy, "Queen of the
Heavens"

Pele* *(Hawaiian)*
Fire, volcanoes

Sarasvati *(Indian)*
Creation, grace,
science, teaching

Vesta *(Roman)*
Fire, hearth, food, chastity

Candlemas Gods and Associations

Bannik *(Slavic)*
Home, hearth

Braggi *(Norse)*
Wisdom, poetry, creativity

Cupid/Eros *(Greco-Roman)*
Love

Dainichi *(Japanese)*
Purity, wisdom

Dumuzi *(Sumerian)*
Vegetation

Esus *(Gaulish)*
Vegetation

Faunus *(Roman)*
Nature, dreams, prophecy, panpipes, Lupercalia, vegetation, woods, cunning

Februus *(Roman)*
Cleansing, February

Nurelli[*] *(Aboriginal)*
Creation, law, order

Prometheus *(Greek)*
Intuition, wise advice, protection, fire, "He who foresees"

Spring Equinox Goddesses and Associations

Aphrodite *(Greek)*
Love, beauty, health, healing

Astarte *(Canaanite)*
Fertility, love

Athena *(Greek)*
Wisdom; courage; war; protectress of architects, weavers, sculptors, justice, smithcrafters, business, creativity

Coatlique* *(Aztec)*
Moon, earth, spring planting festivals

Demeter *(Greek)*
Earth, abundance, fertility, barley, magick, wisdom

Ēostre/Ostara *(Teutonic)*
Maiden, beginnings, dawn, Easter

Gaia *(Greek)*
Earth, fertility, love, business, divination, heartbreak, marriage

Hera/Juno *(Greco-Roman)*
Home; hearth; moon; Mother; protectress of women, marriage, peace, newborns; peacock for Juno, pomegranate for Hera

Iris *(Greek)*
Communication, Messenger of the Gods, rainbow, new endeavors

Isis *(Egyptian)*
Love, Mother, beginnings, moon, disk and horns

Maia *(Greek)*
Spring, rebirth, creativity, May, flowers, green, creation

The Muses *(Greek)*
Inspiration, spring, memory, poetry, creativity, new endeavors, luck

Persephone *(Greco-Roman)*
The Underworld, rebirth, the dead, change, pomegranate, wisdom

Renpet *(Egyptian)*
Seasons, spring, eternal youth

Venus *(Roman)*
Spring, vegetation, love, ocean, "Star of the Sea," Mother, joy, Queen of Pleasure

Spring Equinox Gods and Associations

Adonis *(Greek)*
Beauty, vegetation

Attis *(Persian)*
Vegetation

Cernunnos Herne *(Greco-Celtic)*
Hunt, vegetation, magick

Dagda *(Irish)*
Magick, war, art, strength, music, wisdom, fertility, abundance

Dylan *(Welsh)*
Sea

Great Horned God *(European)*
Hunt, vegetation

Loki *(Norse)*
Trickster, cunning

Mercury/Hermes *(Roman/Greek)*
Communication, travel, speed, Messenger of the Gods

Mithras *(Greco-Persian)*
Light, purity, victory, sun

Odin *(Norse)*
Father, war, magick, poetry, the dead, cunning, creativity, divination

Osiris *(Egyptian)*
Vegetation, fertility, reincarnation, crafts, justice, power, growth, stability

Pan *(Greek)*
Vegetation, nature, woods, cunning, dreams, prophecy, panpipes, Lupercalia

Xochipilli[*] *(Aztec)*
"Flower Prince," corn, fertility, love, dancing, music, youth

Beltane Goddesses and Associations

Aphrodite *(Greek)*
Love, beauty, health, healing

Artemis *(Greek)*
Ruler and source of water, moon, protectress of girls, good weather for travelers, courage, magick, healing

Cybele *(Greek)*
Caverns, mountains, earth in its primitive state, crescent moon united with the sun

Diana *(English)*
Hunt, athleticism, courage, wild beasts, moon, forest, abundance, heartbreak, liberation, success, wisdom

Erzulie* *(Vodun)*
Love, Triple Goddess, exuberance, generosity

Flora *(Roman)*
Nature, flowers

Frigg/Freya *(Norse)*
Love, sexuality, war, protection, peace

Gwenhwyfar *(Welsh)*
Ocean, wisdom, balance, Triple Goddess, royalty

Ilamatecuhtli* *(Aztec)*
"Old Princess," fertility, death, Milky Way

Ishtar *(Babylonian)*
Earth, fertility, battle, storms, marriage, moon, divination

Maia *(Greek)*
Spring, rebirth, creation, May, flowers, green, creativity

Prithbi *(Hindu)*
Fertility, earth, grounding

Rainbow Snake* *(Aboriginal)*
Water necessary for life, menses, justice, magick

Sheela-na-gig *(Irish)*
Great Mother in primitive form, protection, creativity

Xochiquetzal* *(Aztec)*
"Precious Flower Feather," all possibilities, beauty, joy, moon, love, marriage, art, singing, dancing, spinning, weaving, marigolds

Beltane Gods and Associations

Baal *(Phoenician)*
Fertility, vegetation, storms

Cernunnos/Herne
(Greco-Celtic)
Hunt, vegetation, magic

Cupid/Eros *(Greco-Roman)*
Love

Faunus *(Roman)*
Vegetation, nature, woods,
cunning, dreams, prophecy,
panpipes, Lupercalia

Freyr *(Norse)*
Fertility

Great Horned God *(European)*
Hunt, vegetation

King Arthur *(Welsh-Cornish)*
Hunt, wise counsel, leadership

Lono *(Polynesian)*
Fertility

Manawyddan *(Welsh)*
Sea

Odin *(Norse)*
Father, war, magick, poetry,
the dead, cunning, creativity,
divination

Pan *(Greek)*
Vegetation, nature, woods,
cunning, dreams, prophecy,
panpipes, Lupercalia

Puck *(English)*
Cunning

Telipinu * *(Hittite)*
Fertility

Summer Solstice Goddesses and Associations

Aestas *(Roman)*
Midsummer

Aine *(Irish)*
Moon, meadows, Midsummer

Artemis *(Greek)*
Ruler and source of water, moon, protectress of girls, good weather for travelers, courage, magick, healing

Athena *(Greek)*
Wisdom; courage; war; protectress of architects, weavers, sculptors, smithcrafters, business, justice

Eos/Aurora *(Greek)*
Day, youth, beauty

Erce *(English)*
Fruitful womb, early name for Mother Earth

Gokarmo* *(Tibetan)*
"She of the White Raiment," Mother

Hathor/Tiamet *(Egyptian)*
Pleasure, joy, love, music, dancing, beauty, responsibility, friendship, creativity, moon, marriage, art, prosperity

Hera/Juno *(Greco-Roman)*
Home, hearth, moon, Mother, protectress of women, marriage, peace, newborns, peacock for Juno, pomegranate for Hera

Isis *(Egyptian)*
Love, Mother, beginnings, moon, disk and horns

Kali *(Hindu)*
Destruction and death necessary for rebirth, justice, power, protection for women against violence

Marici* *(Tibetan)*
Power, day's first ray of light

Nut *(Egyptian)*
Sky, stars, early morning, womb, dead

Sekhmet *(Egyptian)*
War, sun, Divine order, fierceness, power

Zoe *(Greek)*
Life force

Summer Solstice Gods and Associations

Apollo *(Greco-Roman)*
Sun, strength, courage, creativity, health, healing, heartbreak, justice, knowledge, intuition, success

Baal *(Phoenician)*
Fertility, vegetation, storms

Dagda *(Irish)*
Magick, war, art, strength, music, wisdom, fertility, abundance

El *(Hebraic)*
Father, life cycles, fertility, water

Gwydion *(Welsh)*
Music, reincarnation, vegetation

Helios *(Greek)*
Sun, riches, enlightenment

Jupiter *(Roman)*
Faith, vitality, joy of living, business, confidence, prosperity

Mars *(Roman)*
War, courage, strength

Maui* *(Polynesian)*
Sun, fishing, fire

Oak/Holly King *(Anglo-Celtic)*
Expansion and growth, withdrawal and rest

Ra *(Egyptian)*
Life-giving sun, wealth, power, fertility

Sol *(Greco-Roman)*
Sun, "Unconquered"

Thor *(Norse)*
Sky, thunder, hammer, working class, justice, legalities, Thursday, strength, marriage, protection

Xiuhtecuhtli* *(Aztec)*
Fire, sun, "Lord of the Year"

Zeus *(Greco-Roman)*
Father, power, protection

Lammas Goddesses and Associations

Cabria *(Phoenician)*
Primordial Mother, mystery

Ceres *(Roman)*
Corn

Chicomecoatl * *(Aztec)*
Maize, rural plenty

Frigg/Freya *(Norse)*
Love, sexuality, war,
protection, peace

Habondia *(German-Celtic)*
Witch, abundance

Hani-Yasu-No-Kami *(Japanese)*
Earth, substance

Ishtar *(Babylonian)*
Earth, fertility, love, battle,
storms, marriage, divination

Libera *(Roman)*
Wine, fertility

Mama Alpa * *(Incan)*
Earth, harvest, abundance

Nisaba * *(Chaldean)*
Grain harvest

Saning Sri *(Japanese)*
Rice, harvest, abundance

Tea/Tara *(Irish/Hindu)*
Star, education, ocean, sun,
wishes, happiness, harmony,
healer of sorrows, protection
from fears and suffering

Tuaret *(Egyptian)*
Protectress of pregnant women

Lammas Gods and Associations

Athtar *(Phoenician)*
Sun

Bes *(Egyptian)*
Merrymaking; music; protector of families, marriage, children

Bran *(Welsh)*
War, blessings

Dagon *(Phoenician)*
Agriculture, especially corn

Ebisu *(Japanese)*
Labor, fish

Ghanan* *(Mayan)*
Agriculture

Liber *(Roman)*
Virility, fertility, vineyards

Llew/Lugh *(Welsh/Irish)*
Sun, war, skill, art, smithcrafting, knowledge, "of the long arm" or "of many arts"

Odin *(Norse)*
Father, war, magick, poetry, the dead, cunning, creativity, divination

Xochipilli* *(Aztec)*
"Flower Prince," corn, fertility, love, dancing, music, youth

Autumnal Equinox Goddesses and Associations

Akibimi *(Japanese)*
Autumn, change

Chang O *(Chinese)*
Moon, reincarnation, new moon

Demeter *(Greek)*
Earth, abundance, fertility,
barley, magick, wisdom

Epona/Rhiannon
(Celtic-Gaulish)
Mother, horse, abundance,
change, moon, fertility,
health, healing

Harmonia *(Greek)*
Harmony

Lakshmi *(India)*
Good fortune, prosperity, beauty

Modron *(Welsh)*
Earth, abundance,
fertility, barley

Morgan *(Welsh-Cornish)*
Water, magick

The Muses *(Greek)*
Inspiration, memory, poetry, luck,
spring, creativity, new endeavors

Nikkal *(Canaanite)*
Abundance

Pomona *(Roman)*
Dove, peace, apples, fertility

Persephone *(Greco-Roman)*
The Underworld, rebirth,
the dead, change,
pomegranate, wisdom

Rennutet *(Egyptian)*
Nourishment

Snake Woman *
(Native American)
Transformation

Sophia *(Greco-Hebraic)*
Holy wisdom found within

Autumnal Equinox Gods and Associations

Bacchus/Dionysus
(Greco-Roman)
Vegetation, fertility, revelry,
wine, reincarnation

Great Horned God *(European)*
Hunt, vegetation

Haurun *(Canaanite)*
Healing, death and rebirth,
protection from wild animals

Hermes *(Greek)*
Messenger of the Gods,
communication, trickster,
commerce, travel, knowledge

Hotei *(Japanese)*
Laughter, happiness

Mabon *(Welsh)*
Hunter, fertility, reincarnation

Orcus *(Roman)*
Death, the Underworld

Thoth *(Egyptian)*
Wisdom, writing, communication,
divination, magick, inventions,
commerce, healing, initiation,
success, truth

THE
CRAFT

Talking about the Craft

The word *Witch* still scares many people—that's what centuries of fear and a negative associations with the term will do. *Witch*, as well as the word *Wicca*, comes from the Anglo-Saxon word *wicce* (pronounced *wee-cha*, with a soft *cha*), which means "wise" or "to bend or shape," particularly the shaping or bending of unseen forces.

Wicca is a way of life, an approach to living. Like other earth- or nature-based religions, it teaches that all energy and light comes from the Divine source and pulses through every rock, flower, person, animal, mountain, and body of water. We are all a part of the harmony and rhythm of nature, and the cycle of birth, death, and rebirth. Followers of the Wiccan or Witch path seek to find balance within themselves and to build a connection with nature. As long as you Harm None, Wiccans and Witches are accepting of all different paths to Spirit. You can be a Christian Witch, Jewish, Hindu, Baptist, and so on. We are all here to teach, learn lessons, and experience life.

No doubt about it, some people are interested in Wicca only because they want to learn spells and feel powerful. While Wicca makes you feel empowered, it also connects you to a protective, unconditional force that is your origin. Study the Craft and learn how nature and spellwork can manifest your dreams, bring you unshakable confidence and resourcefulness, as well as harmony to all.

You choose your path, but it also chooses you. So, why be a Witch? There are many reasons for choosing to become—or, rather, awaken— the Witch within you: when you ask a question of the Universe, you will receive an answer; you will feel a sense of belonging; you will have crystal-clear moments of peace, serenity, and connection with yourself and those around you; there is a magnetic force drawing you to the Old Ways and nature. Wiccan teachings illustrate that you are the light. You have responsibility over your actions and you should be able to take full credit for your achievements—there are no failures, only lessons to learn and moments to experience. Spirit wants nothing more than to support you as you experience the joys and the struggles along your Path, and to see you flourish, blossom, and grow. You've come home.

Be it friends or relatives, before you tell anyone that you are interested in or are already practicing the Craft, assess their ability to understand its philosophy. When I was first writing *The Wicca Cookbook: Recipes, Ritual, and Lore*, I took writing drafts to my writers' critique group. Without asking anyone what they thought about the subject, I passed out my samples. The next week, one of the women looked at me with a horrified expression and said, "I can't review this for you." Hearing this, another woman breathed a sigh of relief and said, "Yeah, it scared me just to read it." At first, I was hurt and shocked. It took a while for me to get in the right frame of mind to pick up writing again, but it taught me to consider my audience's ability to embrace certain levels of the topic. Now I do a jewelry check before I say anything. If they are wearing a gold cross, I'll ease in by first framing my work as seasonal living or using ancient traditions such as Celtic lore to explain. The important thing is to keep the integrity of the Craft, but there is no need to scare anyone; all that does is perpetuate negative stereotypes.

Another thing to remember is to keep it sacred. If you start blabbing about a spell you have cast before it has had a chance to materialize, it is like poking a hole in a balloon. The air or energy will leak out, and instead of being able to float out to the ethers and bring back your dreams, it will just weaken and fade away. It's like when you have a great dream. Of course, you want to share it; it was so fabulous, and you believe that by sharing, you can make it more real. But what happens is the opposite. Each time you share the dream, a little bit of the sequence, the colors, and the details become muddled. Instead of making it more tangible, it begins to lose its essence and magick.

TOOLS OF THE CRAFT

This is the fun part: the tools, materials, instruments, and elements of power to utilize in rituals. It is important to remember that while tools help you focus, your intention and integrity are the driving forces behind every magickal incantation.

Some tools you may want to include are an athame (ritual knife used for ceremony), bells, a Book of Shadows (journal of spells, rituals, or dreams), a boline (knife reserved for cutting herbs), a besom (broom), a burin (engraving tool), candles, cauldrons, a chalice, crystals, drums, gems, herbs, incense, jewelry, pentacles, rattles, runes, statues, swords, tarot cards, and wands.

You can get many of these items in metaphysical or earth-based spirituality stores, natural food markets, and even online if you don't have access—however, it is always best when you can make your selection based on by what feels good in your hands. When you buy your tools, never haggle or attempt to bargain over the price, as it is considered bad form and will diminish the tool's power. Some tools may be drawn to you and some as a gift or exchange, but some will be difficult to find, such as astrological oils or dragon's blood. The waiting and searching will serve to sharpen your intention, which is a very helpful thing.

Often your tools can be made from items found in nature. For example, brooms have traditionally been made from rowan, oak, ash, or birch trees, while wands come from hazel, oak, or apple branches. Although these are the most common tree branches and considered the most powerful, you can make a broom or wand out of whatever is available or sacred to you. If possible, pick branches that have fallen on the ground. If none have fallen but some are hanging, ask for permission and direction on which branch to take. Your hand will be guided to the branch, flower, or whatever part of the plant or tree that nature wants you to have. When you take from nature, it is wise to ask permission and always give thanks.

When you begin spellcasting, remember you don't need to have every tool and material listed in order to make magick. The most important thing is to gather tools with intention and purpose. In fact, it is best to begin simply with a few tools so that they become familiar and you understand the symbolism they each represent. My high priestess, Connie DeMasters, often said, "The goal of any magickal practitioner should be to cast your spells and do your magick without a single tool but your conscious intention." Magick is the craft of applying yourself—this is a form of dedication and commitment to your self-evolution. Spiritual knowledge is obtained through practice and determination.

Once you have acquired your tools of choice, you must cleanse them of past energies and fill them with your unique power to make them yours. Charge your tools by performing the following consecration ritual on a night that feels special to you, such as a full moon. In time, you may come up with your own consecration ritual or choose to modify this one as you see fit.

Mix spring water with sea salt in a chalice or cauldron. Sprinkle the salted water over your tools and say:

> **By the elements of water and earth,**
> **I cleanse and bless this (name your tools)**
> **With my pure intent.**
> **By My Will So Mote It Be.**

Light a stick of incense, preferably cinnamon, eucalyptus, or frankincense. Wave the perfumed smoke over your tool and say:

> **By the elements of fire and air,**
> **I cleanse and bless this (name your tools)**
> **With my pure intent.**
> **By My Will So Mote It Be.**

Use your tools regularly, and soon they will be charged with your individual power. You may also want to create an altar for your tools. An altar can be a dresser, nightstand, television tray, table, windowsill, shoe box, or anything that works and feels right.

CHAKRAS

Chakras are energy centers located along your spinal cord. Below you will find each chakra's Sanskrit name, color, location, corresponding element of nature or Spirit, and specific function or benefit. Chakras represent a multitude of emotions, concerns, or obstacles that intersect at that function. Meditations and visualizations often use the chakras to bring power, balance, and energy to that area of your body and life.

ROOT CHAKRA *(Muladhara)*

Color: Red

Element: Earth

Location: Found at the base of the spine, also known as your perineum

Function: Helps ground and center you. It is a source of action, vitality, balance, solidarity, survival, manifestation, focus, connection to ancestors and family, and rules over what we possess in the world.

SACRAL CHAKRA *(Svadhisthana)*

Color: Orange

Element: Water

Location: Just below the belly button

Function: The center of fluidity, change, individuality, motion, nurturance, and sexual intuition and pleasure. It is the place where the duality of our feminine and masculine energies unite.

SOLAR PLEXUS CHAKRA *(Manipura)*

Color: Yellow

Element: Fire

Location: Between the navel and the diaphragm

Function: The center of will, laughter, joy, anger, passion, transformation, power, fortitude, and energy. It is the fire in your belly and the source of gut intuition.

HEART CHAKRA *(Anahata)*

<u>Color:</u> Green

<u>Element:</u> Air

<u>Location:</u> The center of your sternum

<u>Function:</u> Connect to relationships, gentleness, innocence, acceptance, balance, loss of ego, *prana* (the breath of life), and the Universal Love.

THROAT CHAKRA *(Visuddha)*

<u>Color:</u> Blue

<u>Element:</u> Sound

<u>Location:</u> Throat

<u>Function:</u> Controls creativity, order, language, eloquence, communication, and the transformation of thought into words. This is where you tap into your self-expression and connect to yourself and others.

THIRD EYE CHAKRA *(Ajna)*

<u>Color:</u> Purple

<u>Element:</u> Light

<u>Location:</u> Slightly above the space between the eyebrows

<u>Function:</u> Guides inner sight; it is the center of non-dual perception, imagination, intuition, awareness, healing, and nonverbal communication.

CROWN CHAKRA *(Sahasrara)*

<u>Color:</u> White

<u>Element:</u> Thought

<u>Location:</u> Top of the head

<u>Function:</u> Connects us with Spirit and works as a passageway for Divine understanding and knowledge, cosmic consciousness, connectedness, organization, and information.

The chakras work in harmony, with specific connections between the root and crown, sacral and third eye, and solar plexus and throat. Get in tune by lying still and visualizing a spinning flower of light energy in the corresponding color of each chakra. Begin with the root and slowly move upward. Meditate on each chakra and feel its power.

ANIMAL TOTEMS

Another inner instrument of power lies in your connection to animals. Each of the animals listed below offers a gift or source of power for you. When you find an animal that calls to you, you will find a friend, a comrade in good times and bad. If you are not sure who your power animal is, turn to page 120 for the spell and ritual.

Bat
Brings rebirth, power to overcome obstacles, knowledge of past lives, inner strength, fortune, and happiness

Bear
Brings insight, introspection, inner knowledge, healing, prophetic dreams, and increased intuition

Beaver
Brings resourcefulness, security, achievement, hard work; is a builder

Buffalo
Brings prayer, abundance, strength, potency, and alertness

Butterfly
Brings self-transformation, beauty, harmony, ever-changing cycles of life, and joy

Cat
Brings self-assuredness, independence, healing, love, and a sign that you can and will land on your feet

Coyote
Brings cunningness, trickster medicine, humor, shape-shifting, and opportunity

Crow
Brings justice, Divine order, law, shape-shifting, cunning, boldness, and prophecy

Deer
Brings spiritual knowledge, patience, unconditional love, gentle courage, dreams, psychic power, graceful strength; leads us to the land of Faerie or other worlds

Dog
Brings loyalty, love, camaraderie, devotion, alertness, truth; is territorial

Dolphin
Brings playfulness, manna (bread of life), intelligence, deep wisdom, friendship, trustworthiness, eloquence, balance, and harmony

Dragonfly
Brings illusion, magic, dreams, wisdom, enlightenment, and truthfulness

Eagle
Brings spiritual transformation, wisdom, keen sight, connection to Divinity, and courage

Elk or Stag
Brings stamina, passion, endurance, patience, and camaraderie

Fox
Brings camouflage, cunning, intelligence, shape-shifting, and wisdom

Frog
Brings cleansing, transformation, fertility, and release from holding on to emotions

Grouse
Brings connection with the sacred spiral dance of creation and Divine presence

Hawk
Brings communication, magic, observation, transformation, strength; is a Messenger of the Gods

Horse
Brings power, freedom, stamina, friendship, journeys, and faithfulness

Hummingbird
Brings joy, love, possibilities, and happiness

Lizard
Brings dreams, stillness, guidance, and clarity

Moose
Brings self-esteem, wisdom, stability, and accomplishment

Mountain Lion
Brings leadership, fierceness, power, and grace

Mouse
Brings scrutiny, inconspicuousness; is detail oriented

Opossum
Brings diversion, strategy, and cleverness

Otter
Brings female creative energy, magic, joy, friendship, playfulness, generosity, and curiosity

Owl
Brings wisdom, dreams, shape-shifting, keen insight, clairvoyance, and magick

Porcupine
Brings innocence, humility, playfulness, trust, faith, and gentleness

Rabbit
Brings hidden teachings, quickness of thought and action; tends to bring our worst fears the forefront while giving us quiet strength and comfort to conquer our fears

Raven
Brings magic, shape-shifting, spiritual messages, eloquence, and prophecy

Salmon
Brings wisdom, inner knowledge, faith, fertility, journeys, magick, and endurance

Skunk
Brings respect, charisma, and integrity

Snake
Brings sensuality, change, creation; enables you to release old habits; and represents the seven chakras, or energy centers, within your being

Spider
Brings harmony, the gift of weaving, infinite possibilities, beginnings, and fate

Squirrel
Brings abundance, thoughtfulness, gathering, harmony, patience, endurance, and balance of work and play

Swan
Brings grace, power, femininity, dreams, dignity, intuition, and knowledge

Turtle
Brings fertility (as it represents the womb of the Mother), Goddess energy, creativity, patience, and perseverance

Weasel
Brings stealth, foresight, ingenuity, energy, and adaptability

Whale
Brings record-keeping (the history of Mother Earth), balance, music, vastness, family, polarity, and clairvoyance

Wild Boar
Brings confrontation, resolution, power, cunning, intelligence, defense, magick, prosperity, death, and rebirth

Wolf
Brings protection, knowledge, cunning, intelligence, independence; is a teacher, territorial; and represents the pathfinder

RUNES

The runic alphabet has been used for centuries to symbolize cosmic energies and for divination. Drawing or inscribing these symbols on paper, candles, or other objects and keeping them on your person or in your home can help magnetize the appropriate energies to achieve your goals. This chart outlines the basic meanings and uses of each rune.

Fehu
The Rune of money, property, power. This rune stands for creative power, fertility, and prosperity. Good for helping develop psychic abilities, to increasing wealth, self-promotion, and harnessing the energy of cosmic forces. Divination: Issues concerning money and material values are of concern. Can indicate gain.

Aurochs
This is the rune of physical strength, vitality, wisdom, and healing. Brings understanding of the self. Helps imagination and visualization. Divination: Indicates a strong position. Strength, endurance, and determination will assist you in present situations.

Thurisaz
The rune of self-defense, applied power, and rebuilding after crisis. Helps ward off negative influences and awakens willpower. Good for increasing assertiveness. Divination: A problem or crisis is beginning to surface and you must take action to protect yourself and change the energy.

Ansuz
The rune of communication with Spirit, ecstasy, and inspiration. Aids communication with others, enhances psychic awareness, visualization, and self-hypnosis. Promotes fearlessness and understanding of death mysteries. Divination: Important messages are coming from others and from Spirit. Open to receive them.

Raidho
The chariot rune assists those on a journey, both spiritual or literal. The symbol for justice, ceremony, and magick. Awakens the inner voice and tunes us to earth rhythms. Assists travelers. Divination: You are undertaking a journey, trip, or vision quest that will have powerful results.

Kenaz
The fire rune stands for creativity, sexual energy, and transformation. Brings strength and healing and awakens passion. Opens the door to sexual intimacy and artistic inspiration. Divination: A doorway is opening to a new and inspiring cycle.

Gebo
The rune of partnership, sex, and giving. This rune aids in achieving harmony in any kind of relationship, particularly intimate ones. Brings unity and connection with others. Divination: Achieving balance in relationships is important at this time. Love unconditionally.

Wunjo
The rune of joy and well-being. Strengthens bonds between people. Banishes feelings of alienation. Divination: Positive, optimistic vibrations are beginning to affect you and motivate your life. Peace and happiness can be yours.

Hagalaz
The rune of protection and banishment. Use to dispel negative influences. Helps us evolve and move through difficult times. Brings balance. Divination: Difficulties help bring awareness of inner strength and truth. Be calm and centered and control negative thoughts and influences.

Naudhiz
The rune of deliverance from need or stress. Helps us recognize needs and find ways to meet them. Dispels hate and anger. Opens us to Spirit's help. Helps attract a lover. Divination: Use your limitations as a strength instead of weakness. Times of restraint require extra faith and focus.

Isa

The ice rune stands for the ego and controlling the will. Helps concentration and controlling unwanted influences. Divination: This may be a time of standing alone. Do not let fear rule you. Concentrate and center yourself and you will achieve clarity.

Jera

The harvest rune represents rewards, manifestations, creativity, and fertility. Enhances work on long-term projects. Helps achieve peace, harmony, and enlightenment. Divination: Indicates success coming from your efforts.

Eihwaz

The rune of protection and endurance. Protects against hostile forces and people. Helps us to see the truth and talk to Spirit. Increases personal power. Helps remembrance of past lives. Divination: Stand up for your rights and call upon Spirit helpers and guardians in times of need.

Perthro

The rune of fate helps us understand and recognize karmic lessons. Aids in divination and games of chance. Creates change. Divination: Soon fate will move and change will be revealed to you. Change will help you connect with your life path.

Algiz

The rune of magickal protection is associated with protection, defense, and connection to God. Connects us to guardian Spirits. Strengthens luck in all matters. Divination: You may be in a situation where you need protection and you will have it by connecting with inner strength and Spirit helpers.

Sowilo

The sun rune connects us with our guides and helps attract positive, successful vibrations. Use this rune for winning and victory in all matters. Divination: Success, wholeness, and clarity enhance your life at this time.

Tiwaz

The warrior rune promotes justice, victory, and self-discipline. Helps us develop self-reliance, self-control, and sobriety. Helps in conquering fear and doubt. Divination: A fearless attitude is required now to advance toward your goals. Be strong. Powerful forces reside within you.

Berkano

The Goddess rune rules birth, fertility, and motherhood. Helps bring in nurturing, positive, creative energy. Beautifies and regenerates. Aids in conception, pregnancy, and childbirth. Divination: The birth of a child or a new start in some life area is imminent.

Ehwaz

The horse rune symbolizes a vehicle to take us to other worlds. Enhances trust, loyalty, and marriage. Brings prophetic wisdom and swiftness to earthly affairs. Divination: Influences are coming that will get things moving in a new direction and motivate you. Can indicate an actual move.

Mannaz

Symbol for the self, this rune promotes intelligence and memory, and unlocks the third eye. Good for test taking, studying, or interviews. Divination: Center yourself and think about your own goals first at this time. Self-knowledge, self-discipline, and self-love are the keys to your success.

Laguz

The water rune promotes growth, vitality, and flow. Opens up emotions and helps clear out negativity. Enhances psychic awareness. Divination: A flowing, receptive attitude will have a wonderful effect on your present situation. Pay attention to dreams and insights.

Ingwaz

The rune for gathering energy, meditation, and centering the self. Promotes fertility. Divination: Creativity flows from you and as you gather your energies and resources, you will find new avenues of self-expression.

Dagaz

The rune of illumination and breakthrough brings clarity and inspiration from within and above. Clears, balances, and brightens. Divination: You are about to make a breakthrough in some important area. Truth, light, and understanding are on the way.

Othala

Rune of the ancestors, brings sacred protection to the home. Helps increase wealth and property. Divination: The desire to stick with your clan and harmonize your home is strong. Sometimes withdrawal and healing are indicated.

The Blank Rune

This is the symbol of releasing control and allowing higher powers to guide you. Helps us foster faith and trust in the Universe and connection to our higher self. Divination: Transformation, change, the end of one set of circumstances and the beginning of another. Challenge that brings progress.

TAROT

The tarot is a pictographic language the bridges your logical and symbolic mind. With pictures, colors, and symbols, the cards help bring harmony to your conscious and subconscious awareness. Tarot awakens your hidden powers and provides guidance for where and how you need to grow for the benefit your physical and spiritual human experience.

The tarot consists of Minor and Major Arcana cards. The Minor Arcana offers guidance on everyday experiences. They include four suits (Swords, Wands, Pentacles, and Cups) for each of the numbers one through ten and the court cards (Page, Knight, Queen, and King). Each suit also relates to a deck of playing cards, so you could begin to understand tarot with cards found at home. The suit of Swords corresponds to Spades and relates to the element of air, so messages are linked to thoughts, attitudes, and beliefs. The suit of Wands corresponds to Clubs, the fire element, and invokes your energy, motivation, passion, and purpose. The suit of Pentacles corresponds to Diamonds, the earth element, and addresses finances, material possessions, and career choices. The suit of Cups corresponds to Hearts, the water element, and is in tune with your feelings, intuition, creativity, and emotional connection to yourself and others.

Court cards typically relate to a person, usually yourself or someone significant:

King
Order, status, wisdom, strategy, authority, masculinity, responsibility, discernment

Queen
Image, support, intuition, reliability, presence, femininity, knowledge, refinement

Knight
Action, vitality, passion, impulse, determination, initiation, enthusiasm, advantage

Page
Youth, feeling, service, creativity, devotion, sensitivity, inspiration, contemplation

Numbers can be used in tarot or any manner of spellcrafting.

1 Centeredness, creativity, protection, kindness

2 Duality, imagination, dreaming, sensitivity, conception

3 Manifestation, expansion, education, travel

4 Balance, individuality, originality, tolerance

5 Teaching, communication, flexibility, movement

6 Love, nurturing, compassion, romance

7 Spirituality, mystery, sensitivity, faith

8 Infinity, wisdom, patience, stability

9 Endings, courage, conflict, initiative

10 Beginnings, perspective, manifestation

The Major Arcana represent archetypes found in humanity, nature, and the different phases of life. They represent general characteristics and tendencies, so your own interpretation of the symbolism is the key to understanding how their messages apply to your life. The cards offer a window into your beliefs, help you understand relationships on a deeper level, and provide tools to discover life's direction.

There are many ways to learn the symbols and messages of the Minor and Major Arcana. Each morning, you could ask your guides or Spirit what you need to pay attention to, then choose a card and write down what you perceive the message for you to be. At the end of the day, assess how the symbols and message played out. Try sleeping with a card under your pillow and record any dreams or messages that came to you in the night. Another option is to contemplate each card and write down all the symbols that stand out to you, regardless of what the books may say. This deep, spiritual work must integrate with time; make sure to give yourself a little break in between, particularly when interpreting the Major Arcana. Relate the cards to your own experiences so that what you learn becomes your own.

Below you will find each Major Arcana card's traditional meaning and symbolism, followed by an interpretation when found in a reading. Open your mind to all possible messages, listen to your intuition for what resonates most with your life, and accept guidance from the Spirit World. For recommended tarot and oracle decks, see page 211.

1. The Magician/Magus

The Magician is the teacher who works as a channel or instrument for bringing the wisdom, light, and love of heaven to earth. The Magician holds the power of will, simplicity, individuality, and the act of creating. He walks with awareness, striving to bring balance between light and dark and between all opposites. Be careful not to be manipulative, keep your ego in check, and always teach and guide in service to humanity. Connect with yourself—think it, be it, create it.

2. The Priestess

The Priestess is the guardian of the Great Mystery, the unconscious, the void before creation, dreams, and symbols. She holds the power of stillness and self-reliance, seeks inner guidance and enlightenment from the unknown. The Priestess symbolizes everything that is Divinely feminine—emotion, spiral movement, and intuition. She knows the truth of our own essence and is able to bring this forth into life. Remember that even though you have wisdom to impart, there is always more to learn, more that is unfolding in this expanding Universe. Know that to trust yourself is to trust Spirit.

3. The Empress

The Empress represents Mother Earth's energy and abundance. She attracts opportunities by being receptive. She holds the nurturing maternal instinct, life's cycles and rhythms, beauty, and compassion. She manifests through her connection to unconditional love. The Empress is the essence of the creative force and patroness of artists. She brings life into every situation, has high emotional intelligence, and is pregnant with all possibilities.

Be careful not to smother, be possessive, or make anyone or anything the object of your love. True love is without attachment.

4. The Emperor

The Emperor is the courageous, knowing, and responsible leader. He presents Divine masculinity through his determination to achieve, practice of discernment, maintaining sensitivity, and striving for harmony between opposites. He depends on higher wisdom, guided by the sun, and keeps to his good intentions and valor. This is the archetype of the tough but fair ruler, who represents graceful poise under fire with a firm grip on reality. Don't conquer in vain or become seduced by your own power. Maintain your vulnerability and humility through all your many successes and be certain to use your talents and skills to serve humankind.

5. The Priest/Hierophant

The Priest is the patient protector and caring father figure who heeds and shares the knowledge of the ancestors. A practical teacher and shepherd of lost ones, he is able to align knowledge and reason. The Priest understands duality and sees the wholeness of all things, which makes him a great mediator. Constantly in search of the extraordinary, the Priest guides with an open hand and hopeful heart. A peacemaker, trustworthy, and the keeper of the faith, the Priest knows how to bring spiritual consciousness into the mundane world. Don't become too intoxicated with your own counsel.

6. The Lovers

The Lovers see the beauty in the Divinity that makes life and people so irresistibly wonderful. This archetype is the symbol of heaven and earth reaching out to each other until their ultimate integration, the connection where consciousness and expression manifest. The Lovers encourage trust in intimacy and relationships, increased self-love, and finding peace in your center. This archetype helps us see and find the love that transcends conditions or rules, make decisions based on higher truths and wisdoms, and create a path with heart and commitment. Be careful not to make anyone or anything an obsession and don't get caught in one precise way of seeing and feeling Love.

7. The Chariot

The Chariot holds the power of forward movement and the positive use of self-control. This archetype teaches balance between wild and animalistic desires and strength of the rider, until the rider and the animal become one. The charioteer gracefully and lightly guides the wildness without trying to rein it in too hard, which channels the untamable into vast strength. To do this, the charioteer must trust intuition, treat oneself with gentleness, and allow for a learning curve. With a lot going on, be sure to maintain focus, beware of procrastination, and be attentive to the methods used to attain your goals.

8. Strength

The Strength archetype is the symbol of everlasting infinity, the alpha and omega, beginnings and endings. The just use of will, truth, and endurance represented in this card comes from the cosmos and cannot be deterred. This card also symbolizes the connection between beauty's refinement and the raw courage and strength of the beast. Strength has endured much and must find the courage to walk away when necessary and enjoy the bliss of the moment. Here is the champion of the underdog and warrior whose passion is linked to Spirit. Be cautious of your hot-headedness, learn how to best channel your enthusiasm, and strengthen your core essence in order to create and manifest.

9. The Hermit

The Hermit has their back to the world. Unafraid of solitude, the Hermit walks the path of the Seeker and must do what is right for them, holding a light to show the way for others even if they don't follow. In traditional decks, the Hermit is shown carrying a six-pointed light, which represents "As Above, So Below," the knowedge of the heavens meeting with the feelings and experiences of earth to bring greater understanding. The Hermit often takes the path less traveled and is sought after for their wisdom. From time to time, the Hermit seeks community. Isolation is necessary to learn to trust your inner voice, unique light, and your own guidance before you can ascend to unconditional love and wisdom. Be careful not to become so isolated that you avoid relationships. Let your intuition guide the way.

10. The Wheel of Fortune

The Wheel of Fortune represents blessings, abundance, and the overall good within the world. Often depicted with a single eye, the Wheel of Fortune symbolizes how perceived "good" can come from perceived "bad." All will harmonize for your personal growth and change must be embraced. The four elements are represented and the circle symbolizes the continuity of Life. This card reminds us to enjoy the moment and speaks to the freedom gained from trusting Spirit. Life is constantly evolving, and so are you. The Wheel of Fortune encourages you to move toward a higher vibration in thought and action. It is time to fulfill your dharma (your soul's mission) and karma. Don't become paralyzed by overanalyzing, and don't wait for permission to live your life fully. Learn to let go and be willing to take what comes.

11. Justice

Justice represents our connection to the power of balance, truth, fairness, and harmony. The sword of truth stands in the middle to help discern positive from negative. Light, truth, and awareness of the right path are revealed when Justice sifts through the details. Be clear about what you want to do, and what you can do. Use the higher function of wisdom to make decisions and be a force for good in your actions and choices. Remember that life is fluid and don't become too judgmental or closed off; only then you will lead by example.

12. The Hanged Man

The Hanged Man knows that life requires a sacrifice and utter surrender to Spirit. The word *sacrifice* is derived from the Latin word *sacrificium*, with *sacer* meaning "holy" and *facere* meaning "to make." When you surrender your ego or your baggage, it's an act of making something sacred in honor of what you desire. The Hanged Man helps you simplify, prioritize, relax, and let go of the attachments to outcomes. He holds the space for you to walk unknown paths, heal through crisis, and be an example to others through your humility. He is cheerful and not terribly concerned with mundane details. He depends on Spirit for guidance, fully aware that life is one big cosmic play. He is also compassionate about the suffering of others. Be aware of your talent and procrastination. You can teach others through your ability to see that enlightenment comes in all forms and from every experience.

13. Death

Death is the reaper, universally needed so that growth can occur. This archetype requires you to release old ways of being or thinking that no longer serve a higher good, allowing for the alchemy of your life, just like turning base metal into gold. Death is often depicted wearing a crown, which represents your consciousness. Death will guide you to become more compassionate and empathic and to develop a healthy appetite for appreciating life. Trust that Spirit always renews, always restores. You are a catalyst for change and hold secrets of the Underworld. Be careful of becoming didactic, single-minded, or rigid, believing there is only one right way.

14. Temperance

Temperance holds the power of balance between the higher self with the human self. This archetype helps us see the beauty and light within, and grants the strength and confidence to outwardly become that beauty and light. It is the rainbow and promise of hope. Release others from expectations through a strong centeredness and sense of self, and you will be an amazing and healed healer. Your ability to understand the value of the middle path helps you bring peace to situations where others are being extreme. Be careful not to tip the balance and become all work and no play. You have an ability to obtain and maintain angelic or enlightened awareness—the clarity of an uncluttered mind.

15. The Devil

The Devil is the Spirit of positive rebellion and can represent your ego, or personality. Often chains are depicted in this card, holding us back. Listen to your heart and the wind of your soul to be free. The Devil helps us use external signs to reveal internal realities, be creative and sensual, overturn negative influences using trickster energy, and see the pitfalls in relationships based on power trips, attachment, and self-centeredness. Your personality helps you stand your ground and defend your beliefs, decisions, loves, desires, and dislikes. Unguarded, the Devil represents the pride that will get in your way and the ignorance that will cloud your vision. Stay open to the freedom and ability to explore all possibilities; don't create imaginary limitations.

16. The Tower

The Tower helps you give up what you thought was your identity, what you were supposed to be, so you can be what you truly are. Under the guidance of the Tower, the things you cling to most desperately and believe you must remain attached to fall away. Without all these perceived constants, you are forced to find an inner strength. Your defenses crumble so that the light of truth can strengthen you. The Tower symbolizes the possibility of rebuilding from a sense of your beliefs and continually finding fresh and new ideas—a wanderlust life of consistent, personal evolution. Pay attention to the awareness that shows up through lightning-fast insights and the power of the moment, and you will get through any crisis with your natural courage.

17. The Star

The Star represents a time to let your light shine. Live to your full potential. Relinquish any shame or fear—just be bright. Look inward to find your gifts and bring them forward into the world. Here is the window of opportunity for you to welcome in the sweetness of life. Dream big! Believe you can attain the things you want—all is possible. The Star points to a time for meditation and inner reflection and symbolizes vulnerability and being willing to look deep within. Be grateful for and gracious with the gifts you will receive, for they will be many—both big and small. You've worked through much karma and deserve the rewards. Practice mind over matter and tune into the stars and planetary movements. Be careful not to be impatient.

18. The Moon

The Moon represents the subconscious dreamworld rising to the surface. This archetype gives you the ability to watch emotions move and change and grants you the strength to walk through darkness without fear. The card speaks to the peace and compassion that comes when the feral and tamed aspects within learn to work together in harmony. The Moon represents the emotions, illusions, or undercurrents that affect your daily life. Struggle and sometimes a little pain will arise from evolving and shedding of old ways. Now is the time to deal with your karma and become aware of who you are. Be careful not to get stuck in your past. Separate fact from fiction so you will know when fears or doubts are clouding your vision.

19. The Sun

The Sun represents the glory of warmth and growth. It is the creative force at its finest. It is the harmony and ecstatic joy of dancing amid treasures, the belief and experience of success and prosperity. The Sun symbolizes a time of bounty, abundance, and a deep connection to the healing power of the Universe. Spread your joy and sunny disposition, teach happiness through your example, and encourage others to stand in the warm glow of their own sun. Allow your openness and abundance to benefit all you meet. Be careful of falling into apathy and complacency with an attitude that life will always be easy or "everything is good, so who cares or why try." Appreciate your blessings, continue cultivating and sharing them with others, or else you will get "sunburned" and lose these gifts from the Universe. Maintain your ability to connect with life and others, by allowing your openness and abundance to benefit all.

20. Judgment

Judgment represents the observer, one who can watch without becoming emotionally involved or lost. With the power of awareness comes the freedom and clarity to experience life without limits. Discernment and wisdom are gifts of this archetype. Turn your thoughtfulness inward and develop a kind and loving relationship with yourself. A more centered, balanced you will emerge. With your courage to see things as they are, you can learn from experiences and separate yourself from the pain of ignorance. Listen often to your own counsel and strive for more self-directed action; it will usually be very helpful and specific to your own situation. Don't become overly judgmental or jaded.

21. The World

The World represents a relaxing and rewarding time in life. It is the symbol of the victor bounding into the Spirit World. You have arrived and paid your karmic debts. Now it's time to appreciate life. Dance. Enjoy yourself. There is no separation between your higher self and your worldly self. You are in touch with all that is and see Spirit in all that you create. You can see the Divine in every day, but don't languish forever. There is always more to learn.

22. The Fool

The Fool has absolute faith and trust, almost without fear of consequences, because eventually all will work out. The Fool is willing to embrace all experience and so holds the elements as playthings. The World is her playground. The Fool always lands on her feet or at least views it that way. At the Fool's heart are innocence, openness, and adventure. This archetype is in balance with the earth and sky and holds an immense, trusting connection to all that is and limitless possibilities, with a strong belief in the future. Work on completing tasks and let go of the past.

Herbs are a mainstay for most magickal practitioners and have inspired the pathways of Green Witches, Hedge Witches, and Kitchen Witches. Herbs are medicine and can be used in many forms, such as incense, teas, infusions, essential oils, perfumes, salves, hydrosols, powders, or simply bundled as "smudge sticks" (typically using sage or mugwort). When ingesting herbs, always consider safety precautions and your own personal allergies. Incorporating herbs into spellwork is meant to invoke their magickal properties in the etheric realm, not to replace medical care. Please consult a healthcare professional for any serious matters.

It is important to check your sources when purchasing your herbs or gathering from the wild (beware of pesticides). I recommend buying farm-direct, loose-leaf herbs whenever you can. Unlike those purchased from mass distributors, they will have been harvested and dried within that same year. Farm-direct herbs have more life force and biomass, making for a stronger medicine.

Begin working with one herb at a time, rather than blends or formulas. Getting to know one herb at a time will help you develop an intimate relationship with the plant and clarify your understanding of its effect on your mind, body, and Spirit. Try to grow the herb yourself or research where it grows. Observe as many things as you can from its leaf shape, how much water it needs, and which climate it prefers. All these details point to the living Spirit of the plant and will deepen your magickal herbal work. Eventually, you may discover you have made a plant ally, a reliable friend in the green world that responds when you need help, calling you to your highest sense of self.

You can learn more about herbs through online courses, symposiums, conferences, and volunteer opportunities in your community

Astral Flight/Dreams
Angelica, belladonna, datura, mugwort, nutmeg, slippery elm, violet

Balance/Harmony
Basil, bergamot, honeysuckle, orange, rose geranium, sandalwood, sweetgrass

Calm/Nurturing
Chamomile, ginger, honeysuckle, lavender, nettle, oat straw

Clarity/Clairvoyance
Anise, calendula, frankincense, jasmine, lavender, marigold, mint, nutmeg, mugwort, thyme

Cleansing/Purification/Healing
Basil, burdock, copal, cinnamon, clove, eucalyptus, palo santo, rose geranium, sage, sandalwood

Communication
Anise, iris, marshmallow, slippery elm

Creativity
Clary sage, rue, violet

Grounding/Centering
Juniper, nettles, patchouli, pine, sandalwood, spruce, vervain

Joy
Chamomile, eucalyptus, marjoram, nutmeg, thyme

Love for Others and Self
Basil, bay, calendula, catnip, cinnamon, gardenia, jasmine, lavender, marigold, patchouli, rose, rose geranium, yarrow

Peace
Bergamot, rose, vanilla

Prosperity/Success
Lavender, mint, calendula, motherwort, rosemary, frankincense, basil, bay, chamomile, patchouli, cinnamon, nutmeg, jasmine, vetiver

Protection
Cinnamon, clove, comfrey, frankincense, garlic, hawthorn, marjoram, motherwort, mugwort, red sage, sandalwood, yarrow

Purpose/Clear Direction
Bay, cayenne, coriander, dragon's blood, frankincense, juniper, mugwort, myrrh, oregano, peppermint

Release
Basil, burdock, cinnamon, clove, dandelion, frankincense, feverfew, garlic, ginger, lily, milk thistle, parsley, vetiver, yarrow

Self-Reliance
Ginger, jasmine, juniper, lavender, mint, rose, rose geranium, walnut

CRYSTALS

Crystals are considered beings of light and emissaries of the mineral realm. Like herbs, crystals are alive and want to share the wisdom, protection, and health benefits they possess. They want to help us reclaim our power, transform our lives, and lift us to the brightest light and life we can have. Crystals attract and transmute energy. When you purchase crystals, it is recommended that you buy them in person so that you can feel the energy of the crystal and how it responds in your hand.

When you bring your crystals home, you will want to cleanse them of all former energies. You can do this in many ways, such as leaving them under the full moon, wafting sage or palo santo smoke over them, soaking in salted water, or washing them in a moving body of water such as the sea or a stream. Please also see the consecration ritual for tools found on page 45.

Crystal magick is very specific to the individual and their relationship with each stone and mineral. The following list is organized by the strengths and qualities each crystal possesses. They can be used interchangeably and should be selected based on mutual attraction. Make a connection with each stone and mineral before use. Try carrying a crystal in your pocket and note how you feel.

Astral Flight/Dreams
Kyanite, labradorite

Balance/Harmony
Aventurine, aquamarine
calcite, carnelian, chrysocolla,
labradorite, tiger's eye

Calm/Nurturing
Amazonite, amethyst, angelite,
aquamarine, bloodstone,
emerald, howlite, lapis lazuli

Clarity/Clairvoyance
Amethyst, aquamarine, citrine,
fluorite, hematite, kyanite,
malachite, selenite, quartz

Cleansing/Purification/Healing
Amber, amethyst, aventurine,
garnet, peridot, jasper, quartz

Communication
Amazonite, apatite, calcite,
kyanite, labradorite, lapis lazuli

Creativity
Clear quartz, citrine, kyanite,
mookaite jasper, tiger's eye,
lapis lazuli

Grounding/Centering
Amazonite, garnet, hematite,
jasper, smoky quartz, turquoise

Joy
Citrine, rhodochrosite, rose quartz,
sunstone

Love for Others and Self
Aventurine, garnet, rhodochrosite,
rose quartz, watermelon or pink
tourmaline

Peace
Amethyst, aventurine, blue calcite,
blue chalcedony, blue lace agate,
larimar, sugilite

Prosperity/Success
Agate, aventurine, citrine,
emerald, jade

Protection
Amber, amethyst, black
tourmaline, hematite, labradorite,
onyx, obsidian, pyrite, turquoise

Purpose/Clear Direction
Amethyst, ametrine, bloodstone,
calcite, citrine, garnet, jade,
larimar, quartz

Release
Amber, Apache tear,
chrysocolla, citrine, fluorite,
malachite, obsidian, opal

Self-Reliance
Agate, apatite, amber,
carnelian, citrine, hematite,
lapis lazuli, tiger's eye

THE MOON

Many cultures and religions honor the influences of the moon in their languages and symbols. The moon has a strong effect on the ocean's waves and tides, our bodily cycles, and emotions. Naturally, it also influences your spellwork, and certain intentions correspond with the different phases. The moon is considered feminine and a symbol of the Triple Goddess in some cultures. In its crescent form, it reflects the Maiden stage and new possibilities; when full, it embodies the Mother stage, fruition, and attainment of goals and dreams; when decreasing, it is the Crone in all her aged wisdom. Find out the moon phase when you were born, pay close attention to how you feel during that phase, and practice standing tall within yourself.

New or Dark Moon
With the moon hidden from view, this is the time to gain insight about oneself by making friends with our unseen or hidden aspects. Cast spells for introspection, fresh starts, and new beginnings.

Crescent Moon
When we see the sliver of the moon, it is time to do magick for hopes, wishes, and inspiration. The moon looks like a thin crescent in a backwards C shape and represents the Goddess as the Maiden.

First Quarter Moon
This is the time to consider challenges, decisions, and the steps that you must take.

Waxing Gibbous Moon
As the moon continues to grow, it is time to revisit and refine your intentions so they are most clear.

Full Moon
The moon is round, full, and represents the Goddess as the Mother. This is the time to perform positive works and manifest spells that release your most passionate desires.

Waning Gibbous Moon
Perform magick that shows your gratitude and enthusiasm for life. Seek out new truths or perspectives.

Last Quarter Moon
The moon appears as a crescent in a C shape. Perform spells for banishment and release, rituals for knowledge and forgiveness, and concentrate on the Goddess as the Crone.

Balsamic Moon
Surrender, acceptance, rest, and recuperation are where your magickal intentions should be now.

ASTROLOGICAL SIGNS

Astrology plays a major role in magick. Witches follow nature's cycles and seasons, of which planetary and stellar movements are an integral force. Zodiac signs and full moons can help determine characteristics of people and seasons, but they can also affect your Craft. Perform your ritual or ceremony during the roughly corresponding moon and sign to strengthen your spellwork.

OCTOBER: Libra *(Blood Moon)*
Perform ceremonies for those who have crossed over to the other side and give thanks for their gifts.

NOVEMBER: Scorpio
(Snow Moon)
Perform ceremonies for release from negative energy or bad habits.

DECEMBER: Sagittarius
(Oak Moon)
Perform ceremonies for stability and conviction.

JANUARY: Capricorn
(Wolf Moon)
Perform ceremonies for security and comfort.

FEBRUARY: Aquarius
(Storm Moon)
Perform ceremonies for a bright future.

MARCH: Pisces *(Chaste Moon)*
Perform ceremonies for right action and pure intent.

APRIL: Aries *(Seed Moon)*
Perform ceremonies for the manifestation of the seeds of your desires.

MAY: Taurus *(Hare Moon)*
Perform ceremonies for abundance and new possibilities or beginnings.

JUNE: Gemini *(Dyad Moon)*
Perform ceremonies for balance and harmony.

JULY: Cancer *(Mead Moon)*
Perform ceremonies for gratitude and plan what you will do when your spells come true.

AUGUST: Leo *(Wort Moon)*
Perform ceremonies that incorporate herbs in spells, known as wort cunning (the magickal use of herbs).

SEPTEMBER: Virgo
(Barley Moon)
Perform ceremonies for reaping the rewards of your efforts.

COLORS

Colors vibrate light, and depending on the frequency of this vibration, they will affect our emotions and our spellwork. You can wear a certain color, burn candles in these hues, or just concentrate on light of a certain shade to help bring about your desires.

Red
Passion, energy, will, vitality, power, strength, aggression, courage, life force, health, and achievement

Orange
Spirituality, higher levels of awareness, attraction, mental energy, adaptability, motivation, harmony, encouragement, happiness, harmony, and the southern direction

Yellow
Mental clarity, charm, friendship, communication, success, business, and the southern direction

Gold
Solar energy, prosperity, confidence, and success

Green
Money, calmness, nature, the northern direction, balance, job finding, luck, prosperity, fertility, love, and healing

Blue
Truth, healing, decision making, tranquility, understanding, patience, self-awareness, health, dreams, removal of guilt, and the western direction

Purple
Intuition, divinity, royalty, spiritual communication, ambition, and the eastern direction

Pink
Unconditional love, romance, friendship, and protection

White
Protection, blessings, purity, truth, healing, and meditation

Silver
Meditation, hope, and negation of stress

Brown
Grounding, endurance, stability, home, security, and the northern direction

Black
Unknown, removal of negativity, and banishing

DAYS OF THE WEEK

Each day of the week relates to different aspects of our lives and can infuse incantations with more power. There will come a time when you cannot cast a spell or ritual on the appropriate day, which is fine. Magick is practical, and as long as your focus is pure and strong, your spells will reflect this. Whenever possible, though, correspond the intent of your spell or ritual with the natural powers inherent in the days of the week.

Sunday
Ruled by the sun; oversees friendships, jobs, the healing of Divine power, and intuition

Monday
Ruled by the moon; oversees love, home, family, women, clairvoy- ance, subtle changes, medicine, the ocean, emotions, and dreams

Tuesday
Ruled by Mars; oversees confrontation, battle, athleti- cism, hunting, surgery, physical strength, courage, contests, competition, and men

Wednesday
Ruled by Mercury; oversees communication, computers, learning, divination, teaching, self-improvement, and intellect

Thursday
Ruled by Jupiter; oversees wealth, legal matters, money, materialism, and luck

Friday
Ruled by Venus; oversees love, music, pleasure, joy, and women

Saturday
Ruled by Saturn; oversees terminations, the dead, reincarna- tion, elimination, faith, solitude, self-discipline, self-respect, and banishment

THE FOUR DIRECTIONS

The pentagram, a five-pointed star, represents the four directions in balance with Spirit or Love. If you combine the information here with pure intent, your spells will be more powerful, have more punch, and manifest smoothly. For example, if you cast a spell for inspiration, which is ruled by the eastern direction, you could perform at dawn with incense, a feather or an image of birds, a purple or yellow candle, and altar cloth. Incorporating these elements will strengthen your spell, but you do not need to have them all in order for it to be effective.

If a spell does not come to pass within three weeks, it is not that you did it wrong, it is just not going to happen right now. The Universe (*uni* = "one," *verse* = "song") works in harmony for everyone on this planet. If your spell could harm someone, go against their will, has bad timing, or is just not meant to be, the Universe will scatter the energy before your spell reaches its goal. Remember, the Universe always holds up a mirror to reflect back whatever you send out.

EAST

Element: Air

Rules: Inspiration, new beginnings, wind, mental clarity, psychic work

Time of Day: Dawn

Season: Spring

Season of Life: Childhood

Tools: Thurible (incense burner), wand, bells

Sense: Smell

Animals: Birds, especially the eagle and hawk

Aspect of the Goddess: Maiden

Aspect of the God: Lad

Tarot Suit: Wands

Color: Purple, yellow

SOUTH

Element: Water

Rules: Emotions, the womb, subconscious mind, love, adaptability, calmness

Time of Day: Twilight

Season: Autumn

Season of Life: Maturity

Tools: Chalice or cup

Sense: Taste

Animals: Water creatures and seabirds, especially dolphins and whales

Aspect of the Goddess: Mother

Aspect of the God: Father

Tarot Suit: Cups

Color: Blue

WEST

Element: Fire

Rules: Will, action, power, drive, life force, blood, healing, destruction

Time of Day: Noon

Season: Summer

Season of Life: Puberty

Tools: Athame (ritual knife), sword, thurible

Sense: Sight

Animals: Lion, horse, dragon

Aspect of the Goddess: Temptress, Enchantress

Aspect of the God: Adventurer, Warrior, Hunter

Tarot Suit: Swords

Color: Red, orange

NORTH

Element: Earth

Rules: Growth, nature, stability, money, silence, birth, death, sustenance

Time of Day: Midnight

Season: Winter

Season of Life: Old age

Tools: Salt, pentagram, boline (knife used to cut herbs)

Sense: Touch

Animals: Stag, bison

Aspect of the Goddess: Crone, Elder

Aspect of the God: Sage, Elder

Tarot Suit: Pentacles

Color: Green, brown

THE
SPELLS

Casting the Spells

Whether you call it praying, visualizing, dreaming, or spell casting, the words we speak act as an affirmation to the Universe. Once you send a message through your thoughts or actions, the Universal forces are set into motion. Spells are only as powerful as the intentions and emotions they raise inside you. If you believe the color yellow means courage, then it will call forth that ability for you.

Remember that spells are not a panacea for every problem. They are cast to clear the way for dreams to come true by removing self-imposing obstacles and changing your perspective. Spells are not to be cast on or over someone else and must not go against their will. You can try to help others along, but if you try to haul them out of the situation, they might lose the lesson being offered and walk into the same trap again later, only ten times worse.

Some experienced practitioners no longer need to cast a full spell to actualize or materialize their deepest desires. After all, the tools of the craft are just materials used to direct intention, strengthen intuition, and symbolize desires. The rest is a matter of being patient for the right timing and humble to receiving gifts from the Universe.

If requested to perform magick for others, the recipient will need to purchase the necessary ingredients for you to use so that their energy is embedded, but you must not perform for pay. Instead, they may offer you another form of energy exchange, such as doing your chores or giving you a nonmonetary personal gift.

Once you truly understand you are one with nature and Spirit wants nothing more than your highest good, you will begin to recognize the magick and see the energy flowing toward you. Because we are so powerful, we must be very careful when we direct our intent or focus on anything. You have heard the phrase "Be careful what you wish for!"

Before you cast a spell, remember the Threefold Law ("Whatever you do will be returned to you three times three times three"), and ask yourself these four very important questions:

1. Is it necessary?

Have you tried everything your power to make this dream come true? You need to make the first attempt. Magick that is performed primarily for the sake of boosting your ego will have little power. Second, you must ask for what you want with precise clarity. Yes, it is that simple. Sometimes our angels or guides are just waiting in the wings to be asked. Then you must sit still, be quiet, and meditate. Listen for the small still voice nudging you in one direction or another.

2. Is it what I really need?

You may find yourself fixated on a specific image or set of qualifications for your desire. This mindset sets you up for potential disappointment if your dream comes true, but not in the exact shape or appearance of your wish. Ending spells, prayers, or affirmations by saying, "This or something better," is a great idea to remain open to the possibilities.

3. Will it harm anyone, including myself?

You must be ethical and Harm None, the basic tenant of Witchcraft. Harm is different than hurt. Sometimes it is necessary to experience hurt before a need can be met. It hurts to discover you are being shallow or that you must cut ties with someone, but as you cast off unhelpful aspects of your life, like a snake shedding its skin, your spells will manifest smoothly and quickly.

4. Am I willing to own the responsibilities of the results?

Once you have asked the forces of the Universe to shake, rattle, and roll so you can achieve your wish, you must accept the form Spirit has decided will best fit your need. It is like shaking a tree to get the leaves to fall; you cannot determine where they land, only the intent and energy you put behind your action. Remember, in Spirit anything is possible, including those things we cannot conceive.

Before you begin, you may select one of the following ways to ask Spirit whether or not you should cast the spell.

Take a pendulum (this can be a necklace, a chain with a crystal or other charm, or even a string with a needle attached to the end) and hold the lower end perfectly still. Ask the pendulum to show you a *yes* answer, which could be in the form of swinging back and forth, from side to side, or in a circular motion. Ask the pendulum to show you *no*. Now, mention the type of spell and the desired outcome, then let go of the lower end of the pendulum.

You can ask the question by writing it with your dominant hand. Take three deep breaths, clear your mind of all thoughts, pick up the pen or pencil, and answer yourself with your weaker hand. This will transport you to the land of symbols and intuition.

Or, you may choose to mark several stones with the words *no* and *yes*. Turn the stones over, and closing your eyes, mix them up. This will only work if you really lose track of which stone is which. Ask whether or not you should do the spell, and choose a stone.

The art of transforming a spiritual or mental idea into the physical world is awesome, empowering, and one of life's greatest joys. As your intuition grows, you will come to recognize life's smallest gifts manifesting every day. You will clear the way for desires to come through you smoothly and effortlessly. Good luck, and may the Goddess and God light your path with Love and Light.

CASTING A CIRCLE

Casting a circle is an important first step for spellwork. When you cast a circle, you are placing a magickal ring on the earth. This sacred space is a doorway to your Highest Self, Spirit guides, the Elements, Gods and Goddesses. This is where you will find your power to manifest. You may choose a different way to set your circle, but the following knowledge and guidelines are a great way to begin practicing. Gather the necessary materials ahead of time to help you focus. Be ready, fully present, and connected to your magickal circle.

1. Purify, cleanse, and protect each member participating
Light palo santo, dried sage, or mugwort leaves and let them ember. Use an abalone shell or another fire-retardant container to catch the ashes. Direct the smoke toward yourself in a sweeping motion with a feather or your hand and breathe in. Waft the smoke all around you, imagine all negative energy leaving your aura and immediate surroundings, clearing the way for good vibrations. Send positive energy to your heart. This is where your spells will originate. Pass the smoldering herbs in a clockwise (deosil) direction to the next participant. If you are by yourself, just set the vessel in the center of your circle or altar.

2. Ask for protection from the four directions and your guides or Spirit companions

After everyone is cleansed, hold the smoldering sage in the direction of east. Ring bells and *say:*

> Welcome, guardians of the Eastern Quadrant:
> Element of Air.
>
> Bring us your gifts of inspiration, mental clarity,
> and new beginnings.
>
> We do stir, summon up, and call you forth to
> this ceremony
>
> That you may grant us your protection and wisdom.

Move to the south, ring bells, and *say:*

> Welcome, guardians of the Southern Quadrant:
> Element of Fire.
>
> Bring us your gifts of will, courage, and action.
>
> We do stir, summon up, and call you forth to
> this ceremony
>
> That you may grant us your protection and wisdom.

Move to the west, ring bells, and *say:*

> Welcome, guardians of the Western Quadrant:
> Element of Water.
>
> Bring us your gifts of emotions, connection,
> and compassion.
>
> We do stir, summon up, and call you forth to
> this ceremony
>
> That you may grant us your protection and wisdom.

Move to the north, ring bells, and *say:*

> Welcome, guardians of the Northern Quadrant:
> Element of Earth.
>
> Bring us your gifts of stability, instinct, and
> confidence.

> We do stir, summon up, and call you forth to
> this ceremony
>
> That you may grant us your protection and wisdom.

3. Give an offering to the God and Goddess

Sprinkle offerings for the God such as grain, bread, corn, or wheat, in a clock-wise direction around your circle. Alternatively, you can pass bread around for everyone to eat. Be sure to leave a piece for the God in the center of your circle or altar. As the offering goes around, *say:*

> For the God, we offer once more to the earth.
>
> May the exchange bring our desire to birth.

The Goddess prefers liquids, especially apple or passion fruit juice, which is just like her flowing self. Trickle her offering on the ground in a clockwise direction around your circle, or invite your guests to drink. As you distribute the offering, *say:*

> For the Goddess, we offer once more to the earth.
>
> May the exchange bring our desire to birth.

4. Set up the cone of power

Visualize in your mind's eye the energy you have raised to be like a powerful wind encircling your group three times, then spiraling up toward the moon. Your mind's eye is located between your eyebrows and is also known as the third eye or sixth chakra. As your web of energy and light touches the moon, visualize this cone of power protecting you from negative influences while helping to direct positive energy from Spirit, the Elements, and the Goddesses and Gods to you.

5. Ask for your desire to be met

The time has come to cast your spell. You may find yourself in a semitrance state, feel the tingle of magick, or you may not feel anything special. This is where the Witchcraft adage, "In Perfect Love and Perfect Trust," comes into play. Relax for whatever comes.

6. Give thanks and Close the Circle

When you demonstrate your gratitude, you show proper respect for these great forces you have invoked to aid you, and you deem yourself worthy of any further assistance. Hold hands with any members, and walk counterclockwise (widdershins) around your circle three times. Closing the circle will safe-guard your spells while they incubate. On the first turn, use your intuition to verbally thank the four directions as you pass their stations. On the second turn, invoke your love to verbally thank your guardians and angels for their protection and guidance. On the third and final turn, *say:*

> O circle of power,
>
> By our will, we release thee.
>
> Thank you for your guidance.
>
> Return to your place of power.
>
> By Our Will So Mote It Be!

Make noise: howl, clap your hands, and ring bells to disperse the energy. This part of the ritual is like bursting a bubble or taking a broad expanse of energy and scattering it into a million parts to go out to the ethers and be transformed into your desire.

Although it is not imperative to cast a full circle for every spell, it will focus your intent. At the very least, you must ground and protect yourself before all spellwork and magick may be performed. One method of grounding and protecting begins with taking three deep breaths. Imagine a white golden light at your stomach (solar plexus), descending to the depths of Mother Earth and rising to the highest heavens of Father Sky. Once you feel centered, go ahead and start.

You will get out of a spell exactly what you put into it, including your attention, time, effort, and energy. Focus your intent. Speak your chants clearly and with conviction. Keep your heart open.

THE
SPELLS

Emotional, Spiritual, and Physical Health

Banish
Self-Destructiveness

Self-destructive behavior can be anything from eating disorders to physical self-harm, drug abuse, giving away sexual power, negative self-talk, and all things in between. These patterns of behavior often arise when a person feels out of control. Self-destructiveness can provide a way to escape reality and the unmanageable people or things in our lives. This release is temporary and can easily become an addition—compulsive and progressive.

This is a very important spell due to the intensity of it, so I suggest you cast a full circle. Perform this ritual during the waning of the moon. Inscribe your astrological sign and any personal symbols on a white candle. Anoint it with oil that has personal importance for you, such as astrological oil, an oil made specifically for each astrological sign. Surround the white candle with three purple candles to represent clear vision. Anoint all the candles with clove oil, which corresponds to the planet Jupiter. Jupiter represents faith, the development of vitality, the joy of living, and confidence and will help lift your state of mind. Imagine yourself as a diamond with many facets. These facets are the unique aspects of your personality, talents, emotions, and every part of yourself imaginable. It is your job to keep these facets clean and clear. Divinity is a universal force from which light originates and radiates. When the facets of your diamond are translucent, Divinity/God/Goddess can shine through you. It is not your job to determine how good or valuable your assets are; your job is only to honor them, for they are gifts from Spirit. It is not enlightening, nor do you serve others, when you make yourself small and wallow in unworthiness. You are many aspects of Divine specialness. *Repeat this affirmation:*

I am special.

It is safe to be me.

If possible and safe, allow the candles to burn out themselves. Repeat the affirmation often throughout the following week. Allow yourself to be a channel for all the goodness inherent in your being and the Universe. Be gentle on yourself. There is only one you, and we need you.

Be Seen as You Truly Are

Do you ever feel like absolutely no one understands you? Wouldn't it be nice if just one person could really see you—down to the core of your being, past all the walls and masks you put up—and accept you for all they see? It's certainly not easy to portray yourself as you truly are with so much media influence pushing you to meet unrealistic standards and appear as more than a regular person trying to navigate through life's challenges.

Full absorption into social media can become an addiction, limit your creativity, increase stress, and cloud your sense of self. Take a break from social media for three days prior to this spell. Take some time to journal about how it feels when you unconditionally accept yourself exactly as you are.

As you become more open and accepting of yourself, you will radiate and draw others who are open to receiving your light. We can see seven main colors with the naked eye, but so many more exist on the band of light. This incantation will move you into the ultraviolet rays of being. When you allow someone to see to the depths of your soul, they will reflect the light you reflect from Spirit. Through their eyes, you will see and love yourself beyond measure.

You will invoke Ganesha, the Hindu elephant-headed God of fortune, wisdom, and literature. Ganesha's main gift to humans is the ability to remove all obstacles. Place an image, whether it is a postcard, drawing, or statue of Ganesha, next to a white candle. Inscribe the white candle with your astrological sign, a magickal name for yourself that you chose or was given to you, and/or favorite symbols. Anoint both the white and yellow candles with three drops of either eucalyptus, chamomile, or dragon's blood—all these herbs are associated with Ganesha and removal of obstacles to reveal hidden truths.

Imagine white golden light swirling beneath your feet. Close your eyes and visualize this light entering your body through your toes and coursing through your body until it shines from the top of your head and through each finger. Feel the white golden light move to encircle you like a protective shield. Take three deep breaths. *Say*:

> **Ganesha, I call you forth to me today**
> **To remove the obstacles in my way.**

As you chant, imagine yourself infused with inner peace, balance, and relaxation. See yourself as a clear quartz crystal. Imagine yourself wiping each facet clean, like you would a window.

When all your windows are clean, open your eyes. Thank Ganesha and watch the flame dance, imagining this is you dancing in the pure light of your unique self. When you are ready, snuff the flames.

Deal with Anger

There is a well-known Cherokee legend about a young boy who senses a battle going on inside himself. His wise grandfather helps him compare this feeling to a battle between two wolves. One is evil—he is anger, envy, sorrow, regret, greed, arrogance, self-pity, guilt, resentment, inferiority, lies, superiority, and ego. The other wolf is good— he is joy, peace, love, hope, serenity, humility, kindness, benevolence, empathy, generosity, truth, compassion, and faith. This fight rages on deep inside everyone. The grandson asks, "So which wolf will win?" His grandfather replies, "The one you feed."

Anger is simply passing through you. It doesn't have to define you. Let's get it out!

"The holiest of all spots on earth is where an ancient hatred has become a present love."
—*A Course in Miracles*

Go outside and light a black candle. Focus on the flame; visualize it growing in intensity as you think of something that made you angry. Hold an egg lengthwise so your fingers are wrapped over the point. Grip the egg as tightly as you can, sending all your anger into it (if you hold the egg correctly, it will not break). Continue to let the emotion build as the flame becomes more intense. When you are really worked up about it, throw the egg as hard as you can, and yell, "Be gone!"

Place prayer hands at your heart. Take three deep, calming breaths. Visualize the flame of anger dying out as you gently form your hands around it. *Say*:

> **Anger, you once had a hold on me.**
> **Now I release and set you free.**
> **By My Will So Mote It Be,**
> **Three times three times three.**

Repeat it as many times as you need to. When you are ready, blow out the candle and *say*:

> **Take this hurtful anger away from me.**
> **Purify my thoughts, erase the fury.**

Visualize the remainder of your anger disappearing with the candle flame. Light a pink and a white candle. The pink candle represents self-love, and the white candle represents protection. *Say*:

> **I call forth the powerful love of Divine Spirit**
> **To strengthen my heart and all who come near it.**

The next time you are angered and cannot get to a safe place to perform this ritual, visualize it!

Rise Above Criticism

For some of us, criticism can be very difficult to handle. We may even change our behavior in anticipation of being harshly judged by others. Did you know that criticism is an addiction like any other? The one who is criticizing cannot accept things as they are and feverishly attempts to create the illusion of control and perfection according to their myopic perspective—they have forgotten their infallible lovability. Falling prey to the trappings of criticism, whether you are the critical one or the one who is being criticized, is akin to losing your sense of Universal Love.

Realize this criticism came from a unique, frozen moment in that person's life. You received it at a unique, frozen moment in your life. The dynamics will never be repeated. Life is a dance, with the dancers constantly moving and shifting. Why should you hold on to something that may no longer be true, if it ever was in the first place?

Perform this ritual during a waning moon. Write down every nuance of the criticism on a piece of parchment paper. Highlight what is good or what can be construed as positive. Assess how you can change the negative points into its opposite virtue and write these notes on separate slips of paper. For example, if someone said you are selfish, write, "I am now free to give unconditionally." Tape these positive notes on a mirror, or put them in a desk where you will see them regularly. Take the first list and put it in the fireplace, if you have one, or burn it in a safe bowl. *Say:*

> **I now release the negative**
> **And bring to me the positive.**
> **By My Will So Mote It Be,**
> **Three times three times three.**

You can either bury the ashes or flush them down the toilet.

"Let go of the people who dull your shine, poison your Spirit, and bring you drama. Cancel your subscription to their issues."
—Steve Maraboli

Resist Teasing

"Sticks and stones may break my bones, but words will never hurt me" is one of the biggest fallacies we are taught. Words indeed hurt. Words are one of the most powerful tools and aspects of magick we have. With words, we command attention, divulge our feelings, and communicate our needs. Often teasing words seep into our skin and tear at our self-esteem. Etymologically, the word *sarcasm* means "to tear at the flesh."

Even, if you cast a spell to make a bully go away, you may still have lingering powerful emotions and a victim mentality. This is where your true power lies. You have the ability to stop the pain. You can and will release the negative energy and rebuild your confidence, self-acceptance, or whatever else was damaged in the process.

C ast this spell on a Saturday. Anoint a lace blue agate, a stone that brings peace and alleviates depression, with honeysuckle or iris oil, used to bring joy and relieve stress. Rub the oil onto a white candle for protection. Rub the stone over your heart center, and quietly *say*:

> **Angels, Spirit guides, guardians, and friends,**
> **Take away this pain that seems to have no end.**
> **Grant me the wisdom and strength to see my true light,**
> **I am lovable, worthy, and powered by a love so bright.**

Take a piece of lavender-colored cloth (for inner beauty), and place inside one bay leaf (to remove negative energy) and one teaspoon of cinnamon (for strength). Place the agate inside as well. Wrap the cloth and bind it with silver ribbon. Anoint it with your oil. Repeat the chant and visualize a hummingbird and its shimmering breast. A hummingbird embodies joy, possibilities, and happiness. Watch the flame and imagine that it is burning away all the shame that comes from being teased. When you are ready, douse the flame with a candlesnuffer. Repeat the chant for three or nine days, depending on the seriousness, and always envision the hummingbird. Do not be surprised to see the amazing birds appear.

Find Peace
and Serenity

Do you feel scattered? Do you have too many activities going on? Do you feel like the weight of the world is balancing on your tense and tired shoulders? Signs of an unbalanced life include a straight posture that has grown limp, crashing as soon as your head hits the pillow or becoming an insomniac, a short attention span, and being, uh, crabby (that's the nice way to put it). Some days, there's just too much stimulation. Experts say in an urban environment we are bombarded with 500,000 sources of information and stimulation every day!

lear the clutter from at least one space, be it your desk, closet, or under your bed. Do this ritual in silence. Light a stick of sandalwood incense, or any of the other herbs for balance found on page 65. Waft the smoke over a labradorite stone and hold the stone to your solar plexus, the center of courage and grounding, which is located between your ribs at your diaphragm.

Then lie down or sit. Close your eyes and clear your mind. Hold down your right nostril for one intake of breath, exhaling through your left nostril. Then hold down your left nostril for one intake of breath, exhaling through your right nostril. Repeat this for at least ten breaths. Each time a new thought enters your awareness, turn it into a cloud and watch it leave. Try not to get attached to any one thought.

When you feel calm and centered, view your to-do list, from a distance as if it is not yours. What is the first thing that looks out of place? What is the first thing that jumps out as not really serving your current needs and higher purpose? Breathe deeply three times and *say*:

> **I have the courage to change what I must.**
> **I proceed with perfect love and perfect trust.**
> **I now give to the all-knowing Universe**
> **That which stresses, hurts me, or worse.**
> **I call to me peace and serenity**
> **And release what no longer serves me.**

Repeat this chant every day for nine days. Most importantly, drop the first thing that popped up and clear your busy schedule. Approach each day with calmness, focusing on one event at a time

Lift the Depression Cloak

It is easy to allow depression's darkness to get its viselike grip on your heart and energy level. You may be feeling sad, lethargic, melancholic, and defeated, but the truth is you are still a beacon of Light and Love that originated from a source of power and positivity. Cast this spell to help lift the dark cloak of depression and unleash your inner light that has been there all along.

It is important to note that even though apathy and depression share certain commonalities, they are not the same. Depression is a psychological condition where a person loses interest in daily activities, feels hopeless, and may have suicidal thoughts. Apathy refers to the lack of interest, enthusiasm, or direction. See page 100 for a spell for breaking free from apathy.

Cast this spell on a Saturday during the waning of the moon. Since depression can be incredibly debilitating, take the time to cast a full circle (see page 80) before beginning this spell. You will benefit from calling in the guidance and protection from your guardians and the four directions.

Anoint a black candle with frankincense oil, or any of the herbs for releasing, found on page 65. Pour clear, clean water into a glass or bowl, leaving about two inches at the top. Scoop up a fistful of mud. Focus your depression into the mud. It's murky, polluted, threatening, ominously gray, and foreboding. The mud now represents all your fear, frustration, pain, hurt, loneliness, and so on. Plunk the muck into the clean water and *say*:

> **Depression, release your hold on me.**
> **Be gone! By My Will So Mote It Be.**

Blow out the candle when you say "Be gone!" and toss the water outside. Rinse your hands in a bowl of clean water with either lavender or rose petals.

Depression holds focus on what's wrong with you or your life and makes you believe you can't exist without its dark, menacing cloak. Compassion and kindness for others moves the focus off yourself, and according to the Dalai Lama, creates more joy.

Imagine one small thing that you do for someone you love or even a stranger. Drop three drops of your favorite scented oil onto your hands and breathe in deeply. Now go do something nice for another person. Practice this spell as often as you need and don't be afraid to reach out to loved ones, depression hotlines, or a healthcare professional if the depression becomes something you cannot move past on your own.

Break Through Apathy

Apathy is the terrible sensation of being in a black hole. When you are apathetic, you don't care what happens today or tomorrow; you are numb, spiraling backward through a bleak darkness. You may be fully functioning, but your indifference, lack of concern or drive, and inability to conjure emotions has begun to really scare you or your loved ones.

I believe it is the gentle, fragile souls, who feel the deepest pain are ultrasensitive, and fall into the trap of apathy. They have felt so much pain that they cannot stand it, and they shut it off the best they can. But humans are not meant to be detached and alone. We belong to the world.

Cast this spell on the night of the new moon or on a Friday. Light a green candle, the color of your heart chakra—the most favorable place to begin a much-needed and important healing.

By the light of the candle, make a list on a piece of parchment paper of your favorite childhood activities, especially the silly and timeless ones—running through sprinklers, playing hopscotch, swimming by moonlight, coloring, eating Jell-O with your fingers, picnicking, hiking, or rereading your favorite book. Imagine yourself doing these activities.

Fold your list and place the paper inside a green cloth pouch, about six square inches. Grate half of a crayon from every color of the rainbow into the pouch. Mix in one drop of peppermint oil for its uplifting qualities and one-fourth teaspoon of ginger for release, *chant:*

> **I am the light, I am the love.**
> **I now feel the warmth from above.**
> **I am alive and will begin to feel**
> **All that I need to know I am real.**
> **I am the light from the Mother below.**
> **I am the love, which now will show.**

Tie the pouch with a red ribbon, and place the pouch on your altar next to the green candle. Once you have cast the spell, reach out and make small physical contact with your friends and family for a week. Graze a friend's arm as you pass, hold a parent or a partner's hands, or touch a siblings arm while you talk. Come to your altar every day for a week, take three deep breaths, and repeat the chant.

"Death is not the greatest loss in life.
The greatest loss is what dies inside us while we live."
—Norman Cousins

Heal Your Past

Sometimes when we endure a painful incident, we choose to block it out entirely. Other times, we develop an acute sensitive attachment and force ourselves to review the incident over and over again. Other times we review the incident over and over again. Regardless, if we do not let go of our painful attachment to the event, it will eventually cause us harm. The pain grows until, like a weed, it wraps around the heart and squeezes out all love.

Carrying old hurts with you is similar to living with a constant, dull pain. Now you have become both the victim and perpetrator. Many people hold on to painful situations from their childhood or teen years that determine how they judge and respond to friends, relatives, and even strangers. If you can heal yourself of childhood hurts, as well as the ones that happened recently, you will be a more confident, helpful, and open person.

In his song "Anthem," poet and musician Leonard Cohen says, "There is a crack in everything, that's how the light gets in." You may have also heard that bones become stronger where they have been broken. When we are broken, we welcome in the Light and healing can take place.

Instead of focusing on the pain, imagine the Light entering through your wound and bringing you to higher ground. Eventually, your past will no longer upset you and then you will know the lesson is complete. You will invoke the Chinese Goddess of compassion, Kuan Yin. Mix together one cup of sea salt and six drops of yarrow oil for healing and releasing, and frankincense and myrrh for power. Add oils and a lapis lazuli to connect with calming. Stir in a clockwise direction and *chant*:

> **I, who felt violated or hurt, am no longer that vulnerable person.**
> **My thoughts shall no longer cause the situation to worsen.**
> **I now allow the light of Goddess Kuan Yin of compassion,**
> **Who holds me up and molds me in her loving fashion.**

Put one tablespoon of the bath salt mixture in a lukewarm bath. Soak for at least ten minutes and repeat the chant. Each time you think of any sad or hurtful incident, envision it as a golden crack of Light that shows the beauty that lives within you. Repeat the ritual for three days.

Rid Yourself of Guilt and Shame

Self-imposed guilt and shame are nasty little demons. If you are responsible for causing someone pain, especially deliberately, you must take immediate action to remedy the situation, then let it go. Holding bitter thoughts—even against yourself—takes mental, emotional, and physical energy. It makes you obsessive, angry, and depressed. These thoughts work like poison, contaminating our self-esteem and self-image with debilitating force. Forgiveness of yourself is much easier when you give up the irrational belief that you should have done better. This only fuels your frustration, anger, and hostility.

As the saying goes, "Do not *should* on yourself." Each time you say *should*, it is as if you placed a heavy weight on your shoulders. The load will not make correcting your actions any easier. Always remember you are a blessed and loved child of the Universe who does not deserve nor benefit from self-inflicted suffering.

Practice this little ritual whenever you find the word *should* in your mind and speech. Hold a piece of pink rose quartz, a symbol of unconditional love, in each hand. Tell yourself it is unrealistic to expect that you will always perform in the perfect manner. Remind yourself that everyone is fallible and capable of making a mistake. Whenever a hostile or hateful thought enters your mind, try to be fully aware of the harm that resentment can do to you. See those bitter thoughts rise out of your head like a balloon. Imagine taking a pin to the balloon and popping it—vanquishing and diffusing all its energy and power. See the words explode into a mass of confetti letters and turn into a pale pink light. Watch as the pink light enters your heart center as love for yourself.

Author and speaker Brené Brown has written some of the best writings and teachings on shame and may be another resource for you. When the shame cannot be overcome with the ritual above, prepare a bath with a half cup of Epsom salts and a couple drops of rose geranium oil for self-love and finding balance. Lather up a washcloth and repeat the chant below three times while rubbing counterclockwise over your heart. Imagine the guilt and shame washing away. Then rub your heart three times in a clockwise direction and imagine a pink light flooding into her heart, replacing the weighty shame that does not serve you. Recognize that you are a treasured and loved child of Spirit who is made of Love and Light. *Chant:*

> **Healing power, pure and white,**
> **Darkness be gone, let there be light!**
> **Wash this pain away from me.**
> **I am now whole, So Mote It Be!**

Astral Flight

Astral flight is when your consciousness floats into the spiritual realms where you may meet with other people, see into the future or past, visit parallel universes, or dive deep into an energy grid of light and gain wisdom to bring back to your life.

You can enter a dreamlike state with nebulous intentions or travel along the spiritual highways to sacred points. *Nadis*, also known as meridians, are invisible lines of focused energy through our body. *Nadi* is a Sanskrit word meaning "river" or "stream." It is believed there are anywhere from 72,000 to 300,000 lines in a grid of light that maintains our energy flow or life force known as *chi*.

There are three important *nadis*: the *ida, pingala,* and *sushumna.* The *ida*, on the left side of the body, is white and generally associated with the moon, *prana* (rising vital breath), semen, and Shiva (masculinity). The *pingala*, on the right side of the body, is red and associated with the sun, *apana* (descending vital breath), blood or ovum, and Shakti (femininity). The *sushumna* is in the center of the body and is the highway for the chakras. Connection to the *sushumna* brings supreme consciousness, which can frame your vision with soft, white Oneness Light. These rivers of lights connect at powerful points that emanate and pulse with extreme power and can get blocked and released through acupuncture or meditative rituals.

Mother Earth has similar rivers of lights called ley lines that crisscross the planet. Imagine a hexagonal grid of light that connects sacred sites, such as churches, temples, stones circles, burial sites, holy wells, sacred groves of trees, mountains, and other wonders of this world. Trails of sacred pilgrimages often follow ley lines to holy points of light, such as Mount Shasta in California, the United Kingdom's Standing Stones, or Montserrat Monastery in Spain. This energy grid of light is also depicted as the Flower of Life symbol on page 108.

Cast this spell on Wednesday, which in Spanish is *miércoles* and named after the God Mercury, whom you will be invoking. Mercury is the God of communication and travel and the Messenger of the Gods. You may choose to perform the ritual at the same time as a friend whom you want to speak with on the astral plane. Light six white candles and place in a circle. Place labradorite or kyanite (both stones of astral flight) in the center of a small dish of water. Burn frankincense incense and sprinkle dried mugwort around each candle. *Speak the chant over the water to bless it with your intention.*

> **Mercury, Fleet-Footed God carrying messages across a grid of light**
> **Let us travel these rivers of power and healing through astral flight.**
> **A chant in respect of your communication power**
> **Please grant me astral flight this very hour.**

Get into a comfortable position. Anoint your temples and third eye with the water while staring into the flame of your candles and tracing the Flower of Life. Imagine the sacred core, or *sushumna*, of light and send that light to the molten core of Mother Earth. This cord of light will be your tether as you astral travel. Visualize yourself drifting out of your body. As you ascend through the roof of your house, or up past the trees if you are outside, feel the soft breezes of the night sky. You can either keep tracing the Flower of Life or close your eyes. Follow your meridian lines and ask your body a question, or imagine the earth's ley lines and let them transport you on a sacred journey. Take note of the people, places, colors, sounds, or feelings. Stay as long as it feels right. When you hear a voice or something urging you back to your body, begin your return. Follow the cord back through the skies, the trees, the roof, and into your body. See the white light rise up from the center of Mother Earth, back into the base of your spine and travel up and down from the top of your head. Slowly open your eyes and write any images or symbols in a dream journal. Also, be sure to note your dreams over the next few days.

Forgive Someone

Forgiving someone does not mean you have excused or condoned their behavior. Resentment fosters anger, and anger corrodes the vessel that contains it, so the goal of forgiveness is to let go of a hurt and move on with life.

Regardless of what someone did to you, whether once or maybe a few times, every time you think about the incident it is as if you are reliving it. Your brain does not know the difference. Reliving painful events and situations brings toxins and other pollutants into your body. Your thoughts determine your health—both mental and physical. If you harbor and hold sadness in your heart long enough, it will eventually need to escape and find an outward expression, which can result in serious illnesses and more conflicts.

Try this spell first on small slights or insults, especially those inflicted by strangers—someone who cut in line, a rude salesperson, and so on. Use these events as practice to prepare you for the tougher task of forgiving major hurts.

During the waning of the moon, light a black candle for the banishment of your resentment. Burn frankincense and myrrh incense. Write a letter on a piece of parchment paper to the person who hurt you. Express fully, clearly, and honestly how you feel and why that person's action hurt you and made you angry. You will not be mailing this letter, so you do not have to censor yourself. Finish the letter with the bold declaration that you have forgiven them and you have let the pain go. Fold the letter and allow the wax from the candle to drip on the fold, sealing it. As you do this, *say:*

> **I now forgive and release,**
> **Embracing harmony and peace.**
> **From the pain I am free**
> **To live my life weightlessly.**

Then bury the letter somewhere in your yard or even in a distant field. You can also do the Let Me Live spell found on page 142 in conjunction with this spell for extra oomph!

Only people who are hurting lash out with anger, disrespect, or contempt. With this existing pain, their payback has already begun. Do not attempt to bring on their retribution, or you will only accrue your own bad karma. Forgive them, rise up in consciousness, become Love; Love is the master of karma, Love forgives all.

THE
SPELLS

Knowledge and
Self-Knowledge

Cultivate Your Intuition

To increase your intuition, it helps to cultivate your state of innocence. I do not mean naïveté or inexperience. I refer to an innocence that is a suspension of disbelief, a willingness to be free of judgment, open, and incorruptible by the logical brain. It is hard to make room for magick without being open to the possibility that mystical, unexplainable events occur around us every day.

Innocence relies on a primary ingredient: trust. When you trust your instincts and follow Spirit's advice, the little voice of intuition grows stronger and clearer. It does not develop, per se, because it has always been there, it is just that the channel between you and Spirit becomes less cluttered.

*I*ntuition means "inner teacher." Your inner teacher speaks to you in a quiet, guiding voice. The more you follow its direction, the stronger your confidence will grow. To encourage awareness of your intuition, you need to quiet the endless chatter of your mind and listen and meditate.

Burn a sage bundle or dried loose sage leaves, a great scent for opening a vortex to the world of Spirit. Pass the smoke over a clear quartz crystal and/or labradorite, crystals for developing intuition. Light a purple candle to connect with the Spirit realm. Take ten deep breaths. Do not try to resist or control any distracting thoughts, but allow them to surface. Then release each thought with an exhalation. Concentrate on your breathing. Listen to each breath; exhale and inhale. Then imagine yourself walking into a tiny elevator located near your heart center. Descend in the elevator until you reach your gut, or third chakra. This control center will be where your impressions and instinctive feelings about people, places, and things originate. It may differ for some, but people often find their control center under the belly button. Place your hands at this focal point and *chant:*

> **My inner guidance depends on my trust**
> **To believe all the answers lie within is a must.**
> **I quiet my mind, feeling relaxed and free**
> **I know call upon my intuition to guide me.**

Practice this meditation every day, and within a week, you will begin to hear a quiet voice guiding you. Your intuition is like a muscle that needs to be used in order to grow strong. Trust in yourself.

Instill Self-Reliance

The Dalai Lama often tells a fable of an unfortunate farmer whose horse runs away. Later, the farmer's horse returns accompanied by another horse. When his son rides the new horse for the first time, it bucks him off and he breaks his leg. But then, the army comes by to conscript every young man into service and they spare the son due to his broken leg! Some outcomes, decisions, and actions may seem good or bad at first, but all lead to a higher purpose in the end. It is impossible to judge from the start. Self-reliance is a matter of trusting in your path and being blissfully unconcerned with outside opinions on your life and its many winding outcomes. Life is full of illusions—this is the lesson of the dragonfly. Its iridescent wings remind us to see past these illusions, beyond the duality of good or bad, and onward to the Oneness of all things—the origin of pure Spirit.

Combine half a cup of Epsom salts with a tablespoon of jojoba oil and nine drops of lavender or rose geranium oil for self-love and inner strength. Take a shower and use your salt scrub with a washcloth to metaphorically cleanse and scrub off others' opinions—pay attention to the back of your ears, neck, heart, and base of skull. After you are cleansed, copy this image of a dragonfly and color it, while you *repeat the chant:*

> **Oh, Great Spirit**
> **Earth, sun, sky, and sea**
> **You are inside**
> **And all around me.**

Sprinkle a few drops of rose geranium and lavender oil over your dragonfly picture. There is nothing to prove with a steady knowing that you are okay exactly as you are. Self-reliance is knowing you are Spirit. Anything else is simply an illusion.

Discover Your Unique Gift

Everyone has a special talent, a gift. This is not just a mantra repeated by exceptional people taking pity on others. It may be obvious what gifts your friends and family were given, but you might need a little help uncovering yours.

Perform this spell two nights before the new moon. You will call on the Crone Goddess Hecate, the wise Elder who has been around for some time. She knows how to help you discover, cultivate, and use your gift well. Place half a cup of dried mugwort in a jar and cover with almond oil. Shake the jar to activate the herbal medicine. Light a black candle and *chant:*

> **Hecate, old and wise, powerful and true,**
> **Help me see the gift that is my due.**
> **Empower me to use it with good intent,**
> **So all may benefit from my talent.**

Visualize an older woman handing you a present. Take three deep breaths. Douse the flame. Return to your altar the next night. Shake the jar, light the candle, imagine Hecate handing you a gift again, and repeat the chant. On the next night, the new moon, open the jar and anoint the black candle, then light it. See yourself opening the gift and repeat the chant. Journal about your experience and any wisdom that you hear from Hecate.

Find Your Animal Totem

If there is an animal you have always loved and felt a strong, special connection with, you may already have a clue about your animal totem or Spirit guide, or it may have already chosen you. This could be cat, lion, wolf, dolphin, eagle, hummingbird, pig, or frog. It could also be a mythical beast, such as a dragon or unicorn. Think about the qualities your chosen creature possesses. What can this animal teach you? What gifts of the animal would you like to emulate?

If you don't feel a kinship with a certain animal, or you're just not sure, don't worry. Before you go to bed, take a notebook or dream journal, and *write this incantation*:

> **Guardians of the dream world, I call you to my side.**
> **Reveal my Spirit animal, my protector and guide.**
> **Show me the power, beauty, and grace**
> **In the radiant eyes of my guardian's face.**

Use this incantation to let the guardians of the dream world know you are ready to meet your Spirit animal guide. Be patient; it might not happen the first night, so keep trying. Eventually, you will have a dream in which your animal totem appears—and you might be surprised which animal shows up! I know a very petite, quiet girl whose Spirit guide ended up being a huge male mountain gorilla. All animals have strengths and lessons they can lend us, and some people may have multiple connections. Your animal can be called on to help you in the dream world or give you strength in times of need. Just picture the animal in your mind when in need. For additional information on animal totems, refer to page 48.

Victoria Bearden, astrologer, psychic, and magickal practitioner, generously offered this spell.

Find Your Career Path

Following a magickal path puts us in touch with the infinite creative energy of the Universe and gives us access to manifesting that energy in our own lives. The following meditation is designed to tap into our creative power while still honoring the perfect order of the Great Mystery. This is a lengthy meditation and you will want to record yourself.

Sit in a comfortable position, and focus your attention on your breath. Breathe long and deep on the inhalation, and relax on the exhalation, entirely to its own rhythm. With each inhale, visualize a deep green light filling you. As the light fills your body and begins to spill outward, allow it to become a bubble of light in which you sit. Watch as the bubble lifts off the ground, floating up with you in it. Let your bubble carry you to an unknown destination. When you begin to feel the bubble set down, ask Spirit to blow a breeze on you, which clears your body and mind of any preconceived ideas about what your career or job should look like. Feel the wind blow across and through you; feel the magickal breeze lift away any residual need for control, regardless of how that may or may not match how you are feeling. With this consciousness in place, allow yourself to step out of the bubble, examine your surroundings, and see yourself in a beautiful outdoor garden with a magickal spiral labyrinth welcoming you to begin walking toward its center.

Visualize seven different spots along the labyrinth where small altars rest. As you approach the first, leave on the altar a talent or gift you feel you have to share with the world. Place it on the altar as an offering. Continue on your walk, and as you approach the second altar, notice there is a gift for you. Keep an open mind about what you see there. The gift might be obvious, or it might be symbolic, with a meaning that you will recognize later. In any case, take it and hold it as you continue on your walk. On the third altar, envision a Zen sand garden and a feather. Using the feather, draw a complete circle in the sand, and write the word *job* or *career* in the center. Place in the center the gift you received at the previous altar. As you walk farther and approach the fourth altar, notice that it has photos of all the important people in your life, including a portrait of yourself. Here, offer a prayer that your career be one that harmoniously honors your personal lifestyle and needs, as well as those all of the people you love. At the next altar down the path, notice that there is a small bench, a fruit tree, a small shovel, a watering can, a scroll, and a pen. The scroll is for you to write down all the things you love to do in life. Visualize yourself writing anything that comes to mind, even those things that seem unrelated to a job or career. Beneath the fruit tree, use the shovel to bury the scroll, and water the area thoroughly. Know that the energy of this list will become part of the tree and will eventually come to fruition. Wander the labyrinth further, and at the sixth altar, notice a magickal window, in which different pictures present themselves for your review as you gaze out. Ask Spirit to show you anything pertinent to your perfect job or career. Stay out of your rational mind, and observe whatever you see without judgment. When you are ready, finish your labyrinth walk at the final altar in its center. At this altar is an appointment book. Write your name in the book, with a commitment to accept your highest good. Notice that this book has no time or dates. Allow Spirit to work on its own timetable, knowing that our ultimate big picture requirements may differ from what we think our earthly timetable is. Be open. When you are ready, come back to your green bubble, and let it carry you back to your pre-meditation spot. Open your eyes and feel your Spirit reenter your body, as you return to your present surroundings. *Repeat this chant:*

> **May Spirit close any doors to me**
> **That do not serve my highest good.**
> **Spirit rolls a red carpet before me**
> **To show me what direction to go.**
> **By My Will So Mote It Be.**

Be sure to make notes of any information and symbols that the meditation provided, especially the notes on what you love most to do in life. The most important thing is to trust the magickal process and stay out of your linear mind. Do the footwork, but let Spirit bring the outcome. Know that Spirit will bring you the career that best serves your highest good.

"Knowing what you want is the first step toward getting it."
—Mae West

What's in Your Name?

To speak your name is equivalent to speaking your truth, just like to cast a spell, you must name your desire. When you uncover the power in your name, it will help solidify your inner strength, confidence, and self-awareness. Don't be concerned if your name, like desires, change as you change. Life is not meant to be static but rather ever-evolving.

I was born Jamie Della Wolfgang. When my parents split, I took on my grandfather's surname Martinez. When my stepdad adopted me, I gained the last name of Budd. Then I married and took my ex-husband's name of Wood. After I divorced, I wanted a name that reflected who I am today. *Jamie* means "one who shows the way." *Della* was my grandmother's name and refers to nobility, as in "of the house of." I could have been Jamie Della Mariposa (butterfly) or Luna (moon), but after years of debate, I decided to leave it open-ended and chose my female heritage as my last name.

Where is the power in your name? Look for symbols in your family crest, the translation of your family's surname, or symbols related to your first name. Inscribe these symbols and others important to you on a white candle, or choose a colored candle that most resonates with your name (refer to page 70). Research the general meaning of your name and see if there is a correspondence with an animal or any single word.

You can also make numerological and tarot associations. Count the number of letters in your name or, if your name is quite long, simply use the first letter and find its numerical rank from one to nine depending on its position in the alphabet. To do this, start counting and assign each letter a number. When you reach ten, begin again from one until you have gone through the entire alphabet. So *A* will be one, *B* will be two, *J* will be one again since it is the tenth letter, and so on. Correspond your number with the numerology (see page 55) or tarot archetypes (see page 56) and incorporate these elements into your spell circle.

Light the candle and look into the flame as you contemplate this new information. Put on meditative music, such as shamanic drumming, singing, or running water. Write down key words from your discovery with your least dominant hand—this will help you tap into the subconscious because it is more of a freeform style. Then with your dominant hand, begin to translate and write out the essence of who you are, your gifts, and how your name affects your life's direction. Condense the declaration of your name into one sentence and speak it into the flame three times. For example, "I am Jamie Della, the wayshower of centeredness, creativity, protection, and individuality." Or "I am Kimmy, a royal fortress, the lioness of the meadows, the guardian of mystery, imagination, dreaming, and inner guidance." End by saying, "By My Will So Mote It Be."

See the Elemental Beings

If seeing is believing, then believing begins with acknowledgment. You are a Divine cocreator of everything that comes into your life. All of creation begins with a thought, followed by the spoken word, and then the image takes form in matter. The same goes for elemental beings that exist in their shimmering world, a parallel universe alongside ours. Elemental beings include faeries, imps, dryads, elves, sprites, naiads, dryads, and gnomes in all the four elements of air, water, fire, and earth.

Prepare a very sweet dessert, preferably something with cream or honey in it. As you bake, play faerie music or ring bells or chimes. If you are not a baker, it is okay to get the cookies, treats, or cakes from the grocery store. At sunrise or sunset, take your treats, along with a sprig of wild thyme, outside to your backyard. The best time of day is twilight at Beltane. If you do not have a backyard, go to a place in nature such as a park or even near a window box of flowers. Place any crystals that you have or like on the plate. Ring any bells or chimes and *say:*

> **Calling all elementals from your bower.**
> **Come to me this golden hour.**
> **Come to me on magickal wings.**
> **See the treats and creamy things.**

Close your eyes, place the thyme over your dominant eye, and while repeating the chant, move in the direction where you feel the strongest vibration of light and playful energy. Then be very still and listen—the quieter you become, the more you will hear. You may see flickers of light in corner of your eye or hear twinkles of laughter and ringing bells. The faeries might pinch your nose or leave marks on the ground from their dancing and revelry.

Many years ago on Beltane, when my son, Skyler, was a wee one-year-old, we left a quartered blueberry bagel with whipped cream and honey for the faeries in our backyard overhung with morning glories before heading off to bed. As I drifted off to sleep, I felt a swoosh of wind and a tickling on my outstretched hand. Sparkles of Light beings danced around my bed that night and on my hand, they laughed and gave heartfelt thanks for being acknowledged. So magickal.

Increase Your Bliss Tolerance

One day in junior high school, some friends and I were chatting in the bathroom. As usual, everyone started complaining about how big their butt was, about the zit on their nose, or how stringy their hair looked— the list goes on. For the first time, I looked in the mirror and didn't see any of those things. I was truly okay with my reflection. It was a good feeling, but it didn't last long before I started to feel conceit at my contentment.

Many of us put a cap on how much bliss or joy we can allow in our life, as if we can tolerate only so much goodness. Too much happiness and we start looking for the other shoe to drop or Murphy's Law to kick us some bad luck. It's time to increase our bliss tolerance! Let's see how much bliss you can tolerate. Get cozy with feeling good about life and, most importantly, yourself. Just because there are always improvements to be made, it doesn't need to stop you from allowing yourself to feel peace and bliss today.

Place bay leaves (success), basil (warmth), and rosemary sprigs (remembrance) around a rainbow-colored candle or small candles of each color of the rainbow. Imagine these herbs of success, balance, and self-love are a ring of protection around the candle(s). Set seven stones or crystals to represent the rainbow inside this ring. These stones could be all seven colors or simply stones that are important to you. Light the candle. Pick up the stone that represents your red root chakra and *repeat the chant:*

> I now create a space to fill
> With bliss and happiness through my will.
> Rewards and joys will enter in
> As my light shines from within.

In turn, hold each stone of your rainbow and focus your energy on each chakra one at a time as you repeat the chant. Imagine the light of the rainbow filling you up as your kundalini energy raises from the base of your spine to the top of your head. Write down seven things that make you happy. As you bliss out, notice as the feeling of joy fills your being.

Take Responsibility for Your Life

We literally spend years in the care of others. Those ties are not easily cut. Caretakers can receive immeasurable joy from providing love, guidance, and protection. However, like too much of a good thing, it can also become part of their identity and difficult to let go. Often they don't know who they are without the purpose of taking care of others.

At the same time, those receiving care are in danger of being stuck and immersed in their cozy entitlement, forming excuses to avoid taking ownership of their actions or responsibilities. ("It's not my fault the car ran out of gas" or "I didn't have Internet on the cruise to Mexico so how could I have gotten my work done on time?")

If either side isn't careful, the process of give-and-take can become like quicksand holding everyone in place. Loss of dignity or accumulation of resentment can occur. This ritual is for either party, regardless of which camp they find themselves in.

You will create and bless a handmade arrow to help establish direction and trust your own inner guidance. If you have a tarot deck, pull out the High Priestess card or find an image of her online. She is the embodiment of the mystery, the dark cauldron, and the womb of all creation. Ask for her guidance to bring you a vision of what your life will feel like once you have claimed a balanced amount of responsibility for yourself, your actions, and your survival. This feeling is far more important than anything else.

Set aside a quiet time for the creation of your magickal tool. You may purchase a dowel and sharpen it to a point against cement, such as the sidewalk or a driveway. Or find a skinny branch and whittle it to a point. Tie on feathers and different cloth ribbons: red for passion, yellow for inspiration, white for innocence, and black for mystery.

Imagine the quintessential archer. All the energy goes into pulling back the arrow, focusing on the point where you want to go, and then calmly letting go. Using the techniques found on page 45, consecrate your tool.

I drew inspiration for this ritual from my dear friend and teacher Yeshe Matthews, Priestess of the Mt Shasta Goddess Temple.

Blessing Youthful Innocence

When I first looked back at *The Teen Spell Book*, I felt embarrassed about some of the seemingly frivolous spells and my youthful, hopeful point of view. Back then, I was just exiting my Saturn's Return, a cosmic rite of passage, and about to experience the death of three parents, divorce, and a wavering of my faith. Yet, I stand tall today because of my youthful innocence and the wisdom I gained by going through Saturn's Return.

It takes Saturn approximately twenty-nine years to return to the place it occupied at the moment of your birth. During Saturn's Return, which occurs between the ages of twenty-seven and thirty-three, it feels like the things you relied up lose their value or disappear and most everything you knew as a Truth (with a capital *T*) changes entirely.

S aturn, also known as Father Time, invites you to have faith as you grow deeper into your unique self. There is no point in rushing Saturn, the God of agriculture. You cannot force a tree to grow and you can't force Spirit to rush the right timing. Saturn represents faith, solitude, self-discipline, and self-respect. Whining about being young and unknowing does not humor him—the answers will come in time. He does not heed self-recriminations of what you should have known—the past is gone and must be accepted. This may sound harsh, but can you feel some relief in Saturn's restoration of your original and everlasting innocence?

Set out an indigo or black cloth on a Saturday. On the cloth, place a digital timer such as your phone, black and blue stones or crystals, and a small dark bowl filled with water. Burn copal incense. Take three deep breaths and clear your mind. *Repeat the chant*:

Oh Saturn, Father God of solitude
Grant me a forgiving attitude
To accept folly as timely sense
And bless my youthful innocence.

Set the timer to your current age in seconds and let it count down to zero. As each number passes, recall a moment from that age and send your younger self the blessing of acceptance. Repeat the process as many times as needed, coming up with new or difficult-to-forgive scenarios or until you can't come up with a new memory from your youngest age. I started doing this at fifteen years old, using the microwave to count down. It's one of the many ways I can step back into time and viscerally recall what it felt like at varying ages in order to heal my emotional wounds with self-acceptance. I offer this gift to you.

Own Your Star Shine

We all have a star in the skies, like a twin flame, that reflects our unique star shine. This star is our own personal moon, mirroring back to us all the star shine we are meant to share on the earth through our unique and precious life. This spell is intended to help you understand that you are a being of great Light. The world is incomplete when you shroud yourself with feelings of inadequacy, self-doubt, or false modesty.

"There is nothing enlightened about shrinking
so that other people won't feel insecure around you.
We are all meant to shine, as children do."
—Marianne Willamson

Buy a hand mirror with a broad frame. Glue glitter and small pieces of aventurine, garnet, rhodochrosite, rose quartz, watermelon or pink tourmaline to the frame and/or handle. Paint the words at the top of the frame, "I Own My Star Shine." Pull out the Star card from a tarot deck or download an image of the card online. The Star archetype can deepen faith in your purpose, purity, and brilliance. Anoint the mirror and a white candle with chamomile-infused oil for the herb's successful properties and its aesthetic similarities to a star. Inscribe symbols important to you into the candle. Waft jasmine incense over the mirror and candle.

Light the candle so that the flame, the Star card, and your reflection can be seen in the mirror. Repeat this verse of "Twinkle Twinkle Little Star," as a deeply felt question to your twin flame, your star, your truest, brightest nature. *Repeat the verse three times:*

> **Twinkle, twinkle little star**
> **How I wonder what you are**
> **Up above the world so high**
> **Like a diamond in the sky.**

Acknowledge each positive attribute that your star shine reflects back to you. Do not back down from looking at your light. Then *chant three times:*

> **I am a perfect child of the Universe**
> **I am made of pure Light that I must disperse.**
> **I shine with gifts to share that will bless the world**
> **I own my Star Shine that glows like a pearl.**

Journal all the messages you received as if you are writing a letter from your star to yourself. Keep this letter and reread it whenever you need to remember how very beautiful your starlight truly is.

THE
SPELLS

Love, Friendship, and Family

Find Your People

You may have difficulty making friends, or perhaps the friends you have do not meet your companionship needs. It may also feel like you have grown apart from even your best of friends. Much of the spiritual path is letting go of the need to change others. It is through letting go of trying to keep others from growing that we can truly embrace what is real.

Regardless of who you meet, it can feel like no one understands you, nor you them. The first step to finding your tribe and combating loneliness is an openness and willingness to see any similarities between you and possible friends. The people in your immediate environment are there for a reason: to teach lessons *to* you or receive lessons *from* you.

Sometimes being in a crowd and feeling like no one sees you is the loneliest feeling of all. Cultivate alone time and do not be afraid of the stillness. Make time to meditate outside and be still. In this space, you can tap into yourself, your gifts to offer others, and what qualities you hope to attract in others.

Cast this spell on a Sunday. Sprinkle one-half teaspoon of sea salt in a vessel of water. *Say:*

> **By the pure element of salt,**
> **I clear this water of former energy.**

Ring a bell and place a rose quartz crystal (representing friendship) in the water. Sprinkle one-half teaspoon of nutmeg and one-half teaspoon of cloves into the water. Drop in four sunflower seeds. *Say the following chant three times over the water:*

> **I now release the idea that I am lonely,**
> **Calling forth friends in good company.**
> **By the seeds, spices, and crystals there,**
> **I bring in friends and good times to share.**

Leave the water on your altar overnight. The next morning, water a plant or a tree with the water. Visualize the water hydrating the plant or tree with your intention.

Let Me Live

Sometimes it can seem like others have put all their dreams into you and are trying to live vicariously through you. It's the dad who takes more pride in your scars from the football field than you do. Or the mom who won't stop bragging about you, not realizing the pressure it puts on you. Or the teacher or boss who pushes you harder than anyone else because they believe in your potential.

A feeling of suffocation can also come from a friend, or partner who wants to be identical to you or just doesn't give you enough space. This ritual cuts the invisible cords between you and another person, so that fresh, healthy connections can be made. You are not cutting this person out of your life; you are establishing new grounds for connecting. I consistently cut cords with people, including loved ones, especially if we are arguing and communication has become clouded or unkind.

Ground yourself by imagining your legs and feet are like the roots of a tree growing deep into the earth. Take three centering breaths. Light a white candle for purity and unconditional love. Take a picture of the person or write down an idea, concept, or word that carries an energy that negatively affects you, and tape it on a wall in front if you. Using real scissors, snip the air six to eight inches past your toes and above your head, as you *recite:*

> **Mother Earth below, Father Spirit above, Guardian Angels, power animals, spirit guides and all beings of white light,**
>
> **I call on you to help me cut all cords and ties with (name here) from this lifetime or any other lifetime.**
>
> **I ask that all energetic connections are dissolved and transmuted to unconditional love and forgiveness.**
>
> **I now affirm that we are free and this process is complete. And so it is!**

Focus on your chakras (especially solar plexus and heart). Then take the scissors and cut the air behind your head and neck and repeat the incantation. Take a bath with Epsom salts to release any psychic residue. Do this ritual at about the same time for three days in a row and watch the magick unfold.

Find Love

Love spells are tricky work. At one time or another, we all have had our eyes on the perfect partner for us, or so we thought. The problem is we do not always see the whole picture. Maybe they are the one, maybe they are not, and maybe it is love for a moment, a month, or a lifetime. Regardless, there can be no denying it: Being with a special person feels awesome. It is wonderful to share good times and see them look at you in that way that makes your knees melt and your stomach do so many flips you think you will never eat again.

Spells should not be cast on or over someone else—in other words, you cannot make a specific person fall in love with you, but you can welcome love in. When you cast this spell, you will manifest love to come into your life, but always remember that you need to be confident in yourself and not rely on someone else to fill emptiness inside. Spirit may have a better plan.

Cast this spell on a Friday morning close to or on a full moon. Friday is sacred to Freya, Norse Goddess of Love. Before the dew has evaporated, take the petals from a rose, preferably a pink or red rose. If you do not have roses in your garden, buy a rose and leave it outside overnight. Take a pink piece of cloth about four inches in diameter, and place just the petals inside. Dab a bit of gardenia, rose, or lavender oil behind your ears. When the full moon rises, rinse a piece of rose quartz in saltwater and *say:*

> **I cleanse and infuse this stone**
> **For my energy alone.**
> **Bring me the love I desire**
> **By the will of our higher power.**

Place the stone in the cloth. Bind the cloth with a red string or ribbon. As you do this, *chant:*

> **Freya, your power of love Divine,**
> **Bring me a love that is mine.**
> **Bring him (or her) to me in perfect trust.**
> **Harm to none is a must.**

Carry the pouch with you always. Even sleep with it under your pillow. When a new love enters your life, bury the pouch under your favorite flower, bush, or tree. Then follow up with the Give Thanks for Love spell on page 146.

Give Thanks for Love

Think about the countless people whose love has made your life better. Family, friends, teachers, coworkers, and numerous others have shown you that they love you and care about you. Romantic partners and sweeties have helped you see your own beauty and feel your heart expand. If you have one, your animal companion has shared love with you as well!

Take some time on a Friday to offer gratitude for all the love you have had in your life thus far. Gratitude for love is like the water in a river: you always want to keep it flowing to keep it clean and healthy.

Soak for a while in a hot bath to prepare, with salt, rose petals, and maybe some essential oils. As you soak, release all within you that does not resonate with love. After your bath, anoint a candle that you will offer as a symbol of your gratitude: pink for romantic love, green for community and family love, or white for Divine love. Use rose, sandalwood, and/or lemon balm oil as you run your hands over the wax or drip the scent into a glass jar novena candle.

Pour a glass of fresh, clean water and place it on your altar as an offering next to the candle. Light the candle and *say out loud:*

> **Great Loving Universe, full of magick and miracles,**
> **I give thanks for all the love in my life,**
> **All the moments of kindness and tenderness,**
> **Every caring gesture or flirtatious glance.**
> **I honor the ways that love has shaped who I am.**
> **I am an ocean of love.**
> **I am a vessel of love.**
> **I am a being of love.**
> **I follow my path of love with a grateful and open heart.**
> **May I always walk in the Light of Love.**

After saying this, you might specifically list people by name who have loved you. Try to raise the vibration of love in your heart, visualize it as a glowing orb of light, and then send those beams of light out into the world to those who have loved you and to those who need love. When you are finished, leave the glass of water till the next day, and then offer it to the earth or a plant. This simple ceremony is part of a healthy self-care routine. Repeat it every Friday if you like.

Yeshe Matthews, Priestess of the Mt Shasta Goddess Temple and a mystic who follows where the muse calls her on a lifelong journey of learning and devotion, generously offered this spell.

Find and Be a True Friend

Jan was probably one of my truest childhood friends. There was no pretending or competition in our friendship. We had different interests and were open-minded to learning from one another. This simple acceptance and lack of judgment encouraged me to take risks and be whomever I wanted or needed to be. Because she offered such a tolerance for my quirkiness, I sought to return her gift.

A true friend doesn't put what they gain by being with you ahead of what they can offer you. When you see things from a bird's-eye view and distance yourself from sweating the small stuff, you begin to get a glimpse that we are all one big family, here to help one another. To find a true friend, you must first *be* a true friend. You must cultivate the qualities that you want to attract. A candle loses nothing by lighting another candle.

Cast this spell on a Sunday, the day of friendship. Choose a candle of your favorite color, and anoint it with your favorite oil or flower essence. Light the candle and encircle it with your favorite symbols and images; these can include pictures of yourself, especially those taken in your favorite places or with a particular smile or expression you like. Cup your hands about six inches in front of the candle. Send your energy to the flame of that candle as if you were feeding it your light. *Say:*

> **By the hermetic law of similarity,**
> **This candle now represents my personality.**

Take a yellow candle (yellow because it is akin to the sun and representative of Sunday), and hold it in your hands. *Say:*

> **By the hermetic law of similarity,**
> **This candle now represents a friend's personality.**

Take your candle and light the yellow candle. *Say:*

> **I draw to me a friend loyal and true,**
> **Whom I will trust through and through.**
> **Our bond will grow strong and tight.**
> **By both our wills, let this spell work tonight.**

Watch the candles burn for about five minutes. Imagine what it will feel like to be with this friend. Think about the qualities in a person you most admire. Remember, spells do not always manifest in the form we imagine. Be open and allow your true friend to come through, no matter what the package looks like. Use a candlesnuffer to douse the flames.

Have a Peaceful Breakup

This spell is designed to work for a breakup you know is coming. You may be anxious about hurting feelings, burning a bridge. Maybe you have even put off the separation because of your perception of what may happen. Even if it seems impossible, try to visualize a smooth breakup, a transition into a new level of friendship, or a complete separation.

This spell has two parts. You will call on Kali, the Goddess of death, destruction, and rebirth. Concentrate on her ability to help you separate, as well as her strength in rebuilding. The wild boar also helps with confrontation and gives you strength to stand your ground. The reason you are separating from this person is they no longer have gifts to offer you as they once did, but there is still something worth honoring. For this idea, we will call in Kuan Yin and deer medicine, both of which will help you gain a gentle force and fortitude. Kuan Yin is the Goddess of compassion, boundaries, and illimitable possibilities.

Light an orange candle. Hold two pieces of black tourmaline or onyx in each hand. Visualize a yellowish-orange fire burning in your belly. Focus on all the reasons you need to part from this person. Imagine Kali and the wild boar standing behind you as you hold your position. Hold these thoughts for at least ten minutes. You do not have to stand perfectly still for this part of the ritual. It may work best to pace or involve some kind of movement as you build your strength.

Then sit down and light a blue candle. Imagine Kuan Yin and the deer in all their gentle strength. With fluidity, they can shape-shift a tumultuous event into a calm, soothing parting. Understand that both of you have reasons for the way you are and that neither is right or wrong. Imagine the separation without drama. You do not have to divulge every reason for parting as long as you keep your integrity. Hold these thoughts for ten calm minutes. You may want to include gentle, swaying movements. Now take ten deep breaths and *say:*

> **I part from you this very day,**
> **Releasing you to be in your own way.**
> **Thank you for the gifts you gave.**
> **May our paths be blessed, good-bye I wave.**

Go outside and throw the two pieces of black tourmaline or onyx in opposite directions.

This was by far the hardest spell to write and one of the last ones to come forth—until I had to face it in life. I have confidence this spell will work for you as smoothly as it did for me and will be equally as uplifting. Use it as added protection, but if you are dealing with abuse or feeling unsafe in a relationship, please reach out to domestic violence hotlines and support organizations for advice.

Heal a Broken Heart

Heartbreak often takes us by surprise. When we see a breakup coming, we can brace ourselves and begin letting go in small increments. It is the breakups that come out of nowhere that shatter our confidence and sense of security. In this spell, we will concentrate on releasing the painful experience and building a new foundation for you.

Diana the Huntress is the perfect aspect of the Goddess to call on to rescue your broken heart. Because of her assertiveness and independence, she can be invoked for healing. Whether you choose to seek another partner or remain single, one thing is certain: you are being asked by the Universe to see the world alone again, for whatever amount of time. Diana's strength and grace will propel you toward confidence. She will help you nourish your own soul as you hunt for the new you. Her association with the moon will help you make this a subtle, gentle transition.

This spell will work best if you can get in Diana's backyard: the woods, forests, or at least by a grove of trees. Cast this spell on a Monday. Although there will be things you want to remember about your lost love, some things need to be released before you can heal your heart. Find a symbol of something that brings you a particularly strong amount of pain. For example, this could be a card professing undying love and loyalty sent just before the betrayal, a reminder the plans made just before you were dropped, or a picture of the two of you. If you cannot think of a representation, that is okay. Instead, take a piece of red carnelian and squeeze it to infuse all your heartache into the stone. Obtain a larimar stone, a walnut, a tree seedling that can grow in your area, or wildflower seeds, and a watering can full of water. Next, on a piece of parchment paper, write a letter to your ex. Include all the things that caused you pain and any hurtful things you did not get to say. Sprinkle two drops of yarrow oil, an herb for healing wounds, pulling out poisons, and letting go, on the letter. Dig a hole big enough for your seedling or seeds, the physical representation of your relationship, the letter, larimar stone(s), and walnut. Place all your items in the earth and *say:*

> **Diana, I call you forth. Arise, awake!**
> **Accept these seeds, take this heartache.**
> **By this letter and gem(s) I release,**
> **Calling in your courage to bring me peace.**
> **Use this walnut to strengthen my heart,**
> **For from this pain I shall gladly part.**

Cover with dirt and water.

Help a Friend in Pain

This spell needs to be cast with the purest intent and with an emphasis on what is right for your friend. Sometimes we have horrible experiences so we can learn a lesson, such as how to protect, love, and honor life and ourselves. Sometimes we need to visit the edge before we can see how far down it is to fall. This spell, which will be more like a ritual prayer, can be cast for anyone who is in trouble or experiencing pain of any kind.

The first thing for you to realize is your friend is the only one who can raise themselves out of the pain. Sometimes a person's way of dealing with pain is to lash out or even clam up; most of these actions are survival skills they have learned to help cope and have nothing to do with you. As a friend, you are not required to sit by and be their punching bag, nor should you take it personally. Before doing this spell, be sure to ask your friend's permission to make them a healing pouch, as magick is never performed for someone without their knowledge or permission.

Write down your friend's name on a piece of paper. Write down every wonderful quality about your friend. Fold the paper and place it on a green cloth. Add a piece of amethyst and eucalyptus leaves or oil. As you bind the cloth into a pouch with a silver or green ribbon, *say:*

> **Guardians, protect (friend's name).**
> **Right action takes place.**
> **Help (friend's name) out of this space.**
> **Show them the love around**
> **By Divine will from sky to ground.**

Give the healing pouch to your friend. Even if your friend takes time to process out of their pain, they will feel your support and the unconditional love and that is true magick.

Make Peace with Your Loved Ones

We are all children of the Divine, both Goddess and God. Some see the ocean as a Divine physical embodiment or incarnation, making each of us little waves. Each wave moves in rhythm with the other waves, sometimes big and sometimes small. Sometime, the water rushes back toward the sea, collides with the incoming wave, and shoots into the air, rainbows shimmering and reflecting through the tiny droplets like a million miniature diamonds.

Imagine your family members and yourself as these two opposing waves. You have similarities: both come from the same source, and your makeup is somewhat alike. But your direction, how you respond to life, and your course are different. When you clash, it can be spectacular, or at least loud. We are all doing the best we can to honor our individual natures, even parents. There really is no perfect mother or father; we are all striving.

Perform this ritual during a waning moon, preferably on a Sunday, and if possible, with the family member with whom you are fighting. Fill two glasses with pure water. Put two drops of orange blossom oil in one and two drops of vanilla oil in the other (alternatively, you can use rose oil, bergamot oil, or lemon oil). Pour the two glasses of scented water into a bowl, preferably a vessel special to both of you. As you combine the water, *say:*

> **Waning moon, old and wise,**
>
> **With you this argument dies.**
>
> **Take away the hurt and pain.**
>
> **Reunite (family member's name) and me once again.**

Write down what upset you most—get underneath the anger. If you can, share your feelings with your family member. Dig a hole in the earth and bury the paper with a labradorite stone. Give your pain back to Mother Earth so she can compost it. Pour the water over the mound and repeat the chant.

My mother and I did this ritual when I was forty years old about hurts we had caused each other when I was a teen. There were many tears, but the love was stronger than the sadness. It's never too late to create peace.

Summon a Loved One's Spirit

People come into our lives for a reason, a season, or a lifetime. Some people leave a imprint on our hearts, never to be erased by time or memory. We are blessed to have many people in our lives, even though some of them may have died, also known as crossing to the other side, passing through the veil, transitioning, and by other terms. The use of different phrases is important because it points to the fact that there is a thin veil between those living on earth and those in Heaven, the Other Side, Spirit World, Nirvana, Summerland, Elysian Fields, and many more names. There is a way to move between the worlds and connect with those no longer with us in flesh and bone.

Most of the time this connection will not be in the form of having a chat with our loved one sitting at the end of our bed, although it can be. Often, we will experience their presence. The room may turn cold, the wind might pick up unexpectedly, or we may be surrounded in an aura of color. Since we are all energy, even in Spirit form, often our loved ones communicate with us through electricity. Lights may flicker, computers could randomly turn on, or the phone will ring but no one answers on the other end. You do not need a specific reason to summon a loved one, other than to simply enjoy their presence again. This is not a spell to be done lightly or for show. This is a formal request to pierce the veil between the living and the Spirit realms and must be performed with pure intention.

A great time to do this spell is on Halloween, also known as Samhain, or any Saturday otherwise. Place a picture of your loved one on a north-facing wall, or if you can, position an altar in this direction. Light a white candle. If you know your loved one's favorite scent, either burn that incense, wear that perfume, or place that flower on the altar. If you do not, gather lavender sprigs, wear a few drops of lavender oil, or burn lavender incense. Prepare a snack for the two of you (or however many people are in the ritual), making sure to include your loved one's favorite foods. Sit in front of your altar, and imagine them sitting next to you. Relax; you are only calling on the Spirit of a familiar loved one. Watch for any little sign, which may also come later in a dream.

THE
SPELLS

Protection

Heal from Sexual Harassment

Sexuality is power. Those who are weak and insecure will attempt to steal it from others by any means, namely sexual harassment. All bullies attack as a method of making themselves feel better and filling that dark hole of self-loathing. People who sexually harass others are coming from a weak, vulnerable position and want their victims to feel just as powerless.

On a piece of parchment paper, write the words *sexual harassment.* Around it write every word you can associate with the phrase. When you have exhausted every feeling you have on the subject, fold the paper away from you and seal it with black wax (do this with a wax sealant kit or by dripping candle wax; just be careful not to burn yourself). At the top of the paper, draw a pentacle. You are releasing your attachment to the painful experience, you are recognizing that the offender lacks courage, and you are reclaiming your own power. A pentacle is a five-pointed star in a circle, which symbolizes the four elements in balance with Spirit.

Put the paper in the freezer and *say:*

> **Your harassment now will freeze.**
> **No longer will you provoke or tease.**
> **Find the love in your heart**
> **To leave me be as we part.**
> **By My Will So Mote It Be!**

Place a heavy stone on the paper. After forty-eight hours, more or less, bury the paper or burn it and flush the ashes. You may want to also perform the Empower Yourself spell on page 202 or the cord-cutting Let Me Live ritual on page 142 for additional help in disengaging from this person and the act itself. Please be sure to seek help from loved ones and medical or healing practitioners, and consult legal protection or guidance as needed.

Call for Protection

There are times we feel particularly vulnerable, whether it's in a new environment or a truly dangerous one, and feel the need for some extra protection. Perhaps you are leading the charge for sociopolitical change, or standing up for the underdog (whether that is you or others), or maybe your light is so bright that you have attracted the envy of others. You don't have to explain why to anyone, including yourself. Trust your intuition.

The rune Algiz is the symbol for magickal protection (see page 52). If you feel the need, you can wear a pendant with that rune drawn or inscribed on it to enhance protection. You can also use henna or a permanent marker to "tattoo" Algiz somewhere on your body.

Carrying or wearing black tourmaline, obsidian, black onyx, or rainbow obsidian will also help keep you grounded, aware, and feeling protected. Remember, these stones, symbols, and spells are not an excuse to take foolish risks. Connect with the warrior within to make the right decision. Do not make your guardian Spirits work overtime.

To activate your Divine protection, take three deep breaths. Close your eyes and imagine a golden, multi-petaled flower radiating from your third chakra. Watch it grow with each breath while *chanting three times:*

> **I am protected in front of me.**
> **I am protected to the right of me.**
> **I am protected behind me.**
> **I am protected to the left of me.**

As you sit in silence, watch the golden light begin to shine outside of your body and form a circle of light around you. Hold that image, open your eyes, and step forward into whatever comes next, knowing that you are protected.

Cast Out Bad Energy

Negative energy feels eerie—often cold and kind of hollow. It could be caused by holding negative thoughts or even restless Spirits. Since you have a body and Spirits do not, you have the right to determine the mood of your physical place.

This ritual is called "smudging." It derives from a Native American tradition of purification and protection. You can either choose to buy white sage bundles, readily available from metaphysical and magick shops, or make your own. When wild harvesting, be conscious that you are taking from a sentient being, never take more than one-third of each plant, and leave an offering for Mother Earth, such as water, tobacco, or a crystal. After you have collected about ten sage stems, bundle them together with yellow or red thread. Hang the sage upside down in a dry, cool room for a week, depending on the humidity.

On the night of your ritual, take three calming breaths and bring your awareness into the current moment. Go outside to the farthest eastern corner of the property you live on. (If you prefer to have more privacy, you can do this in your room or house.) Light the sage bundle, and blow out the flame until the leaves ember. Use a feather (a turkey feather works best) to direct the smoke away from you in a sweeping motion, and use an abalone shell or other fire-retardant container to catch the ashes. Decorate these tools by tying beads, special stones, or other talismans to the end of the feather or shell. *Chant*:

> **I cast out negative energy this very night.**
> **I am protected by Spirit's power and might,**
> **Surrounded and embraced by pure love.**
> **As it is below, so it is above.**

Move in a clockwise direction until you have blessed and protected all four corners, and then go into your house. Again, beginning in the east, direct the smoke to every high corner, around every window and door, and over every drain and toilet. You may also ring bells or shake a rattle for extra protection. Nature abhors a vacuum, so when the smudging is complete, burn honeysuckle, rose geranium, or sandalwood incense to bring in peace and harmony. This ritual will clear your house of all unwanted energy and prevent negativity from entering your home, while it seals in positive energy.

Release Someone Who Has Harmed You

This is a ritual for blessing and releasing someone who has harmed you. They may have ruined your reputation, caused physical harm, bullied you in a myriad of ways, or done something that most people would call unforgivable. You may have already cut cords (see page 142) to change the dynamics of your connection, but now you can release them so that your worlds will not intersect. If they do, this person will have no power to negatively affect you and may never even notice you, as if you have become invisible. It's a matter of seeing the Divine at work in all things and blessing this person to move on their path toward Love and Light.

Sit quietly by yourself, and meditate for a few minutes to clear your mind. Just close your eyes and follow your breathing. When doing visualization work, you must be alone, relaxed, and somewhere private. Doing this on the beach or at a park could work if it is not crowded, you know no one will disturb you, and it is a safe place to be. The idea is no distractions.

When you are relaxed and peaceful, with your eyes closed, picture a blank movie screen in your head. The movie begins when you see the person you wish to release. You are now in the movie too, standing right in front of that person. Look them in the eye, and with love in your heart, *say this to them:*

> **I bless you and release you.**
> **You are now free to walk your path**
> **And follow your higher good without me,**
> **As I am now free to follow my own path.**
> **Now go in peace.**

Put your hands on the person's shoulders, turn them around, and watch them walk down a beautiful country road until you can no longer see them. You can open your eyes. You may find that if the attachment to the person is particularly strong, you have to repeat this process several times before it works. This is not a spell to do if you are temporarily mad at anyone. Only do this if you are really serious about not having this person in your life anymore—it works.

Solve Legal Matters

There are many ways to run into trouble with the law. If you have legal matters, consider it an opportunity to learn a lesson regarding rules, stability, orderliness, faith, continuity, and responsibility. Perhaps you were born to break the rules for more inclusion and fairness—your job may be to instill kindness back into humanity.

The intent of this spell is to sway judicial decisions in your favor. If you have committed a crime, this spell will not relieve you of your karma. But you can hope to achieve a lighter sentence by a confession of anything unethical through a willingness to settle up with the Universe. Your compliance and readiness show courage, and that will be rewarded. If you have found yourself in a legal battle, have faith in Jupiter and stand firm in your innocence. Jupiter rules legal matters, and this God cannot imagine losing; he embodies the essence of faith, vitality, and confidence.

Cast this spell on a Thursday. Light two brown candles for grounding and anoint them with Jupiter or rosemary-infused oil. Place them on either side of a white image candle that has been anointed with your astrological or favorite oil. Grind two tablespoons of rue (the name of this herb originates from the Greek word *reuo*, which means "set free"), the petals from three marigolds, and three sprigs of chamomile or dandelion with a mortar and pestle. While you grind, *say:*

> Law and order, be my friend.
>
> Justice and balance on the mend.
>
> Turn the legal battle in my favor,
>
> For it is victory and peace I savor.

Sprinkle the herbs in a purple cloth, and tie with a gold ribbon. Repeat the incantation. Take the pouch with you to court or whenever you are discussing this legal matter.

THE
SPELLS

Productivity

Show Me the Money!

Prosperity is your Divine right. Your willingness to embrace prosperity is a spiritual manifestation of the wealth of the Universe, equally available to all of us. This spell was created for those of you who have difficulty attracting and managing your money or resources. Money has only the significance that we give it—otherwise it is just pieces of paper and metal coins.

Cast this spell on a Thursday, which is ruled by Jupiter, who oversees wealth and material gain. The optimum time of day to perform this ritual is six hours after sunrise. Obtain several pieces of prosperity crystals, such as green tourmaline, turquoise, tiger's eye, or citrine. Green tourmaline also represents the ability to transform negativity into positive situations. All crystals carry multiple healing qualities. For the purpose of this spell, you will be invoking turquoise as a master healer. Tiger's eye brings balance, while citrine is known as the merchant's stone. Light a green candle to represent money and an orange candle to symbolize divinity. Write the amount of money you need on a piece of paper (you do not need a million dollars; remember, magick is practical and should be taken seriously). Put nine juniper berries and three sprigs of sage in the paper. Wrap with a gold ribbon and place on your altar.

While chanting the incantation below, place the stones in a bowl of water with a teaspoon of sea salt. After you take the stones out, waft lavender, patchouli, and Jupiter incense around them. Wire-wrap or bead the stones into a necklace, bracelet, earrings, key chain, or whatever suits your creativity. Every once in a while, look into the flame of the candle, and when the creation is complete, *repeat the chant:*

> **Jupiter, judicious God of prosperity,**
> **Teach me the joy and wisdom of money.**
> **Abundance is my Divine right.**
> **Prosperity is in my sight.**

Keep your prosperity amulet near or on you. This will not only help you draw prosperity, but it will keep it coming and help you spend it joyously as well as wisely.

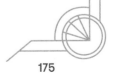

Have a Good First Day

Whether it is school, work, or moving into a new community, everyone wants to experience a good first day. This spell is intended to help you have a great new beginning. One of the most important aspects of being happy anywhere is attitude. If you wake up and say to yourself, "This is a bad day" or "I hate Monday," and so on, then no amount of spellwork will help you. You color every event in your life by your outlook and the way you approach it. Your attitude determines whether or not you will get off on the right foot for a fresh start.

Know that every day is in harmony within the Divine order. Harmony begins as an idea or thought, eventually manifesting into your actions and character. Perform this ritual the night before your big day or at the beginning of a new phase of your life. Anoint a light green candle with the essential oils of violet (prophetic dreams, creativity), vetiver (prosperity, repels negativity), sweetgrass (peace, unity), peppermint (change, healing), orange (abundance, happiness), eucalyptus (protection, purification), and basil (banishment, sympathy). Repeat the word *harmony*. Concentrate on the images of harmony as you chant. Place aventurine (beginnings), amethyst (clarity), and Apache tear (transmuting negative to positive) crystals around your candle. Light the candle, imagine a positive outcome, and *repeat this chant:*

> **Through Divine harmony, I now bring to me**
> **A blessed new beginning of my destiny**
> **By My Will So Mote it Be**
> **This I make true, three times three times three.**

This candle magick was offered by my cousin Kelle, an eclectic green witch by ancestral calling and magickal candle maker. She works with herbs, crystals, and oils with powerfully positive intention to create everyday magick.

Land the Job

Jobs allow us to earn money to pay bills, create independence, give us purpose, and hopefully feed our passions. You need to put your best foot forward when applying for the job of your desire. Be sure to dress appropriately, be articulate, and follow through.

C reate a list of all the attributes that you want your dream job to have, such as mentorship, flexibility, upward mobility, creativity, stability, pride in ownership, a specific field of study, right/left brain balance, salary specifics, and so on. These are feasible, tangible things that you can do on your end. The power and direction of every spell begins with you doing everything you can physically do to bring about your desires.

Cast the spell during the waxing of the moon, preferably on a Thursday. You will need three colored candles: green for opportunity, yellow to bring in your desire successfully, and red for action (because you probably needed the job yesterday and would like this spell to work as quickly as possible). Burn money-draw incense or sprinkle rosemary leaves around your candles. You will anoint each candle with pine oil for success. Review your list of dream job attributes as you rub the oil on your candles. *Chant:*

> **Bring this rewarding job to me**
> **On the wings of serendipity.**
> **The money and opportunity**
> **Will bless all completely.**

Light the candles and repeat the chant three times. Allow the flame to burn for at least ten minutes before dousing with a candlesnuffer. Read over your list and don't worry about when or how the job will appear. The most important aspect to focus on is how you want to feel when this spell has manifested. After the completion of the spell (and all others) comes the time to let go and allow the Universe to bring you your highest good.

Make Peace with Authority

There are times when we are going to run into authority figures who do not like us—it is inevitable. Sometimes we can just remove ourselves from the situation, and other times it is a situation that needs to be endured by both parties. In life, we will encounter oppressive authority and people who enjoy manipulating and controlling others. On the other hand, some of us just have a rogue personality that can't stand *any* form of authority, oppressive or not. Many subcultures and legends are born from this independent streak, from musicians to rock climbers to entrepreneurs and beyond.

Try using a pendulum to assess whether this is a manhole you can walk around or a hurdle you must jump over. Ask the pendulum to show you *yes*, which could mean moving back and forth or around in a circle. Ask the pendulum to show you *no*. Ask if you can leave the situation. If the pendulum shows you *yes*, then proceed with this spell.

Cast the spell on a Wednesday (the day that rules communication), and if you can help it, do not do this during a Mercury Retrograde, which confuses communication and often causes spells to backfire. This spell should be cast with an intent of building peace, harmony, and communication between you and this authority figure.

You will be invoking Brigid, the Irish Goddess of fire and inspiration. Burn a purple candle for intuition and Divine law. Remember a particularly bad incident with this authority figure. On a piece of parchment paper, draw symbols that relate to the incident or write out the whole scenario. Wrap an amethyst, the stone of healing, peace, communication, and anger management, in the paper. Seal it with wax from the candle, being careful not to burn yourself. As you do this ritual, *chant:*

> **Brigid, ruler of the darkness of winter,**
> **Make this harassment break and splinter,**
> **By your light and pure fire,**
> **Befriend (person's name) by mutual will and desire.**

Bury the pouch in your yard.

THE
SPELLS

Self-Improvement

Accept Your Body

Sometimes we pray for obstacles and imperfections to be removed before determining why they are in our lives. Like a diamond, however, if we did not have little nicks and unique facets, our light would not be as brilliant. An uncut diamond can be dull and plain, but one that has a multitude of curves, edges, and slants, like the many features of our bodies and personalities, is beautiful and brilliant to behold.

E arly in the morning, before the dew has evaporated from the grass and flowers, ask permission to take the petals from one fresh rose (preferably pink or red). Light a pink candle. You may choose to cast a circle or set a sacred space by imagining you are one with all the goodness of the Universe. Fill an ice cube tray with fresh spring water, and place one petal in each cube space. Place the tray in the freezer.

As you do this, reflect on the idea that your body is a diamond and the vehicle for your Spirit to share your Divine essence with the world. As you learn to accept and appreciate this hardworking body exactly as it is, you can begin to see how your Spirit and body are working in perfect harmony. Your acceptance works like polish on each facet of your unique being, so that you radiate wherever you go. When the water has turned to ice, place the cubes in a glass of pink lemonade. Reflect on turning your bitterness (like lemon juice) about your body to sweet love (like the rose petals). Drink this beverage every day for one week at your favorite time of day and *say:*

> **I accept my body.**
>
> **I accept myself exactly as I am.**
>
> **I accept the person I am growing to be.**

Soon you will learn to honor everything about yourself that makes you a blessing to the rest of us.

Be Brave and Invoke Courage

Building your courage begins with little steps. You can use this spell for a variety of reasons: standing up to peer pressure, banishing someone who hurts or intimidates you, or releasing phobias such as a fear of heights or closed-in spaces.

To rid ourselves of fear, we must confront whatever scares us. Fear carries with it a sporadic vibration and grows when we feed it energy. Fear is really an acronym for False Evidence Appearing Real. The only way a fear is going to leave is if you meet it head on. To accomplish this, you must arm yourself with the bravery of going into battle. Courage comes under the realm of Mars, the Roman God of war. And with bravery and courage comes strength of heart, a strong conviction of your rights and confidence.

To give this spell its greatest potency, work on one fear at a time. Begin by journaling why or how this fear has been helpful or harmful. Then write how your life will improve after the fear has dissolved. Cast the spell on Tuesday, as Mars rules that day. Because Mars is known as the Red Planet, anything you can do to bring this color into the incantation would be helpful. Obtain a bloodstone, rhodochrosite, garnet, or ruby. Wear the color red for the ritual. Light a red candle. Anoint the stone with dragon's blood-infused oil. Rub the oil onto the stone, and imagine yourself doing whatever it is you fear. It is not necessary to imagine yourself going above and beyond reasonable expectations. For example, if you want to stand up to a bully, do not visualize the bully in turn being afraid of you. That does not serve anyone's highest good. Just imagine the situation being resolved. As you rub in the oil, *chant:*

> **Mars, God of war and confidence,**
> **Grant me bravery and assurance**
> **To stand up for what is right**
> **By your strength and courageous might.**

It is best to begin with little steps toward bravery to build your confidence and self-esteem. You do not have to swim across the lake, around the pier, or competitively to overcome your fear of water. Carry the stone with you until you have successfully faced your fear. Afterward place it on your altar as a reminder of your courage and the obstacles you are willing to face.

Befriend Your Weaknesses

Spirit presents us with disadvantages as a means of strengthening us. Often these "weak points" turn out to be our greatest strengths because they protect our core selves and offer us the discovery of new abilities that can empower us.

By making friends with our weaknesses, we can turn them into our guardians. If you ignore weaknesses, they can take over, or worse, you may project them onto others, attributing your downfalls to other people. In other words, you will see others as the ones who are flaky, insecure, or obnoxious, when in reality, it is you.

Get three ribbons each about one foot long: white for being centered in the truth, yellow for the courage to come face-to-face with the things you like least about yourself, and red for its power to transmute. Hold the ribbons together and tie together in knot at the top. Burn palo santo and allow the smoke to pass around your ribbons. Braid the ribbons for three inches down from the first knot and then tie another, following with another three inches of braiding before your final knot. As you tie, you are containing your negative thoughts, sending yourself love, and creating an intention to see this aspect of yourself in a positive light. With each knot *repeat the chant:*

> **As I tie this knot, I bind the thought**
> **That I am from the imperfect lot.**
> **I befriend all aspects that I see.**
> **I am made in perfect harmony.**
> **I call my radiance to shine forth**
> **By powers of east, south, west, and north**
> **By My Will So Mote It Be**

When complete, you will have three knots and each one will represent one of your "weaknesses" that you will eventually see as a strength.

You can also use this same knotwork craft to call in desires. When this magickal practice was first given to me, we used three ribbons that corresponded with the colors of each sabbat and made a wish or called out something to release with each knot for the new season. You may choose to leave your knotwork on your altar or tie it to your chalice or ritual cup.

Spell by Connie DeMasters, Elder High Priestess
of the Crimson Dragon Druidic Craft of the Wise

Set Aside Your Shyness

Shyness is common to most everyone in some form or another. One of my best friends is terribly shy but when she feels particularly unsure of herself, she gets loud and boisterous. It is a distraction and avoidance of the real concern, which she readily admits. Others combat shyness with jokes or by withdrawing. Shyness may simply be who you are. You may not ever want to change your shy nature, and I would never want anyone to feel less than spectacular because they have an introverted personality. This spell is for those occasions when you may need to step out of your comfort zone and set aside your shyness for an event, interview, or important conversation.

C ast this spell during the waxing of the moon. Sit in front of a white, unlit candle, and take three deep breaths. Imagine yourself as a confident mighty oak tree that is completely stable, powerful, and calm. Once relaxed, light the candle and visualize the flame opening up your heart chakra. Envision your heart opening as a pink rose unfolding its petals. See the brilliant color spilling out into the world. Picture a flood of pink light flowing from your heart and mingling with the white energy from the candle. Visualize the white candle as another person or group of people, your energy mixing with theirs in conversation, laughter, and partying. You are separate yet together.

Repeat this chant:

> **I welcome the new into my life.**
> **I step forward fearlessly and without strife.**
> **I have many gifts that I can bring**
> **To any occasion, let this truth ring.**

Ring bells and repeat this affirmation as many times as you feel necessary. Practice speaking to the candle as if it is someone you are meeting for the first time. Feel the warmth of the candlelight as a response to the gifts you are bringing to the conversation. Finish your conversation and say "See you later" to the candle, while putting out the flame. Repeat this spell as often as you wish.

This spell comes from Myrddann, a Wiccan High Priest and Ordained Minister of the Progressive Universal Life Church.

Find Grace and Style

We grow in spurts and bursts—whether that is mentally, emotionally, or physically. Maybe you developed a sudden awareness of a habit, a new attitude, started a new job, or you realized that a person no longer serves your highest good and you're ready to drop it all like a hot potato. Or, physically, perhaps you've just lost weight, gained weight, or grown taller. To truly integrate the information, awareness, a new body, or new way of being, it's most helpful to make the transition as smooth and graceful as possible.

As you cast this spell, wear dark blue and use as much of the color as you can with candles and stones—especially lapis lazuli and flowers (even some lavender)—to evoke Goddess energy, which calls forth nurturing, balancing vibrations. Notice, too, that blue is the color of the throat chakra, and the swan is well known for its graceful neck. You will concentrate on the purity and elegance of the swan, the archetypical animal of grace and style that is particularly sacred to Aphrodite, Venus, and Sarasvati.

Arrange your blue sacred objects in a semicircle around a picture of a swan. Light a blue candle. Hold the lapis in your hand. Close your eyes and visualize yourself surrounded by gray mist. You are a swan—beautiful and graceful, gliding across a woodland pool. The sky turns from indigo to a pale blue. The last star disappears as the sun kisses the horizon. The sun's first light pink, orange, and yellow colors dash across the sky. The morning mist turns into a silvery veil that lifts all around you as it ascends toward Heaven. You continue to glide effortlessly and poised with grace and style. *Chant:*

> **I now embody style and grace.**
> **Slowing down my rhythm**
> **To swan's smooth pace.**

Open your eyes and watch the candlelight. Repeat the chant nine times over the next three days. Carry the stone with you until you feel swan's energy and medicine descend on you.

Learn How to Trust Again

When I was fourteen, my best friend and I got into a huge fight, and she stopped talking to me for months. I was crushed. For nearly twenty years, I shied away from anyone who might call me their best friend. I've known people who were held back a grade and spent their adult lives believing they were stupid and attacked anyone who commented on their intelligence, even if it wasn't insulting. Or others who choose an abusive partner and even after breaking up, decide they can't trust themselves and decide to live alone. By holding on to this limiting self-perception, we cannot accept the treasures in the present moment, and recognize how we have matured. Instead we create walls that keep us from knowing true companionship and friendship.

Cast this spell on a Saturday for banishment. Gather the rose petals from one pink or red rose, two sprigs of rosemary, and one teaspoon of witch hazel. *Write with a silver pen on a piece of parchment paper the following words:*

> **Light, Lord, and Lady,**
> **I surrender to all distrust.**
> **Grant me love,**
> **Grant me peace.**
> **Cut these ties,**
> **This I seek.**

Wrap your gatherings in the parchment paper. Burn the paper in a safe container such as a fireplace, fire pit, or sizable cauldron. Repeat the chant nine times over the next three days. Feel your heart crack open and allow the trust to fill it up.

Release the Trickster

Using double-talk, lies, or clever distractions to avoid trouble or responsibility is called "trickster medicine." The Native Americans call on Coyote or Crow for cunning, the Norse trickster is called Loki, and the English know him as Puck, the mischievous fellow in Shakespeare's *A Midsummer Night's Dream*.

If you fall into this category, you are quite clever. You can make up a lie and make it up quick. You are witty, hardly ever at a loss for words, and as sharp as a tack; little escapes your bright mind. The trickster is definitely a leader or friend on the path back to Spirit.

Trickster medicine can serve us for a short time, cleverly coming up with reasons to escape punishment or retribution. Eventually, all tricksters fool themselves. One day, you will find you have worn the Coyote mask one too many times, and when you look in the mirror, you cannot tell which part is really you and which part is pretend. The key to using this medicine to your benefit is laughter.

Be on the lookout for times you may be fooling yourself. Laugh at yourself. Angels fly because they take themselves so lightly. Release the burdens and trust. The first step is fessing up.

Cast this spell during the waxing of the moon. Sunday is a good day for this spell because it symbolizes maintaining relationships, the sun, and bringing the light or truth to the forefront. Light a blue candle for truth, an orange candle for harmony—which will hopefully ensure there is no sacrifice of friendships due to your tricks—and a purple candle for karma. More than likely, you will have some amendment to make, but using a purple candle will help increase your intuition and allow you to foresee a correction that can make the road a little less bumpy. Include in your ritual pictures or images of Loki, Puck, Crow, or Coyote. *Say:*

> **I now take off the trickster mask.**
> **In the realm of truth, I will bask.**
> **Harm to none, By My Will So Mote It Be,**
> **Three times three times three.**

Lay the image of the trickster facedown, and repeat the chant.

I Am That

The Path of the Witch lives by the power of "I am that." This declaration means, "I am all that I see in the world and all the world lives in me, as me." There is no separation between you and the Divine found all around you. Nature is the teacher and guide to understanding yourself and your intentions. The chill of winter reminds you to go inside and listen carefully to your heart's desires. I am that. The full moon's light illuminates the present moment, urging you to look around and go after your dreams. I am that. The warm sunshine casts rainbows on a drop of morning dew, bringing beauty to even the smallest of things. I am that. You are a part of the Divinity in the natural world and you are exactly who you are meant to be. I am that!

You are sacred exactly as you are. Your personal values, definitions, behaviors, and boundaries are holy. You have the support of all Divinity to actualize "I am that."

This spell will clarify, strengthen, and bring appreciation to your unique light. Place a blue bowl filled with water on a green cloth next to an image of the Grouse, whose animal medicine invokes the sacred spiral that will bring you to your center. Light a yellow candle to represent the third chakra of will and use the flame to light your smudge stick. Welcome the four directions, which you can do based on the directions on page 72. *Journal on these questions:*

> **What are the things I enjoy doing or do well?**
>
> **What are some of my best personal qualities?**
>
> **What are some my unhelpful ones?**
>
> **What are examples of roles, behaviors, or expectations set for me, based on my gender, my sexuality, or my background?**
>
> **What are examples of behaviors or expectations that make me feel upset, angry, or uncomfortable?**
>
> **What are examples of those that fill me with light and hope?**

After journaling, cut up magazine clippings of words and images that represent you and your dreams. Paste the most important clippings in the center of a board, then move downward and out in a clockwise direction, like the spiral dance of the Grouse. Bless your vision board with the smudge smoke while chanting, "I am that." Place the collage where you will be able to see it every day.

"What you seek is seeking you."

—Rumi

This ritual was provided by Colelea, a working-class Witch, poet, activist, and community herbalist. In her spare time, you will catch her talking to plants, staring at the moon, hanging out with her cat, and hiking.

Stop Worrying

Worrying is like paying interest on a debt you may not owe. Thought precedes action. When you weigh yourself down with worrisome, debilitating thoughts, it is as if you entered a quagmire. It will not matter how much you struggle to get through; as long as you worry, you will keep sinking deeper. Write down everything that you are worried about and place it in a special box.

On the night of the full moon, turn on meditative music. Sit comfortably, light a white candle, and place it directly in front of you. Drop three drops of vanilla onto the candle. You can choose to record the following visual meditation and play it back for yourself or just memorize it.

Close your eyes and visualize yourself in a forest glen. Majestic trees of all forms and shapes surround you. There is a myriad of colors: the deep and light greens of the trees, the sky's cornflower blue, and the rich brown of the earth. With each breath, you become calmer and the forest glen becomes clearer and more defined. You may see a forest animal run past. Your angels or other guides may decide to visit. Say hello to your brothers and sisters. Continue to be aware of your breath. Listen to the forest's sounds. You hear a gentle lapping of water. A small pool appears at your feet. Sit beside the water's edge, and look for your reflection. Is the water clear and bluish green, or is it murky and brown? Is your brow wrinkled with worry, or are you smiling? If you are smiling and the water looks pure, hold this image and remember that you can be this person always. If the images are gloomy, allow your fingers to skim the surface of the water. As the rings of water disperse, see a mist forming just under the surface like a tiny tornado. Watch as the mist calmly passes through your image, erasing the lines of despair on your face. A soothing white light rises out of the water and begins to surround you. You are now free from all anxiety, and all the answers will come to you effortlessly and smoothly.

Slowly bring your awareness back to the present by scrunching your toes while still holding the image of yourself embraced by the white light. Watch the white light move through your toes into the earth, flexible enough to travel wherever you go. Allow yourself to feel each part of your body as you come back to the present moment. You are still surrounded by white, cleansing light. Dab vanilla oil behind each ear. On the next full moon, open the box and see how your worries have worked themselves out.

Empower Yourself

There are many times during the course of our lives when we give our power away. When we allow others to judge, humiliate, or condemn us. When we allow these words, actions, or inaction to hurt us, we are giving our power away. No one can take away your power without your permission. One incident can color and inhibit similar relationships for eons, but once you shed light and understanding and gain true perspective, you can live more fully with power and grace. The beauty of this spell is the freedom it gives you.

This process will begin to free you from the associations with the pain attached to any person, situation, or symbol. It does not dictate that they or it will not be in your life. It simply gives your power back, so you can make a conscious decision in your next encounter to be strong regardless of their presence or absence.

Focus on your solar plexus, the center of self-worth, confidence, self-esteem, choice, and power. At some point during the visualization, you may feel intense distractions, but keep going. This is your ego trying to sidetrack you from releasing the pain and connecting yourself to Spirit.

Take three cleansing deep breaths.

See, sense, or feel the person, symbol, or situation with which you have an issue or problem. Personify it. Imagine them or it standing before you. Look directly into their eyes or at the symbol. See the area above their solar plexus and watch it open. See or feel this area open in your own body.

See, sense, or feel all the power you gave them, coming from their solar plexus back to yours. If you need or want to, you can demand your power back with words. Pull all your strength back into your body. If it helps, you can visualize the place where the pain originated. Continue visualizing this stream of energy until you no longer feel the need to or the stream disappears on its own. You have a right to take all your power back.

See, sense, or feel a stream of energy going from your solar plexus to their solar plexus. You are handing back all the baggage you have carried around for them. In this moment, you can also visualize leaving a gift, such as a flower, candle, or seashell. This person, symbol, or situation has given you the chance to learn a lesson, and the gift can be symbolic of ending this cycle. Continue this visualization until there is no energy left to give back.

See, sense, or feel your solar plexus area, and that of the other filling with white light. See the "karmic cord" between the two of you dissolve

and completely disappear. See your solar plexus area and that of the other close shut.

Allow yourself to talk to them. Say all the things you have ever said or wanted to say. Get everything off your chest; literally free your heart's center of all burdens. Now allow yourself to listen with your soul-self when they talk to you. This will feel like you are listening from your heart's center, or at your third eye, or you may even hear their words from a space around your body. Be open to whatever words come through. Let the person or symbol get everything off their chest. Allow yourself to be a channel and do not force the words or assume you know what they/might say.

Now allow yourself to hug or touch the person or symbol in the most loving, healthy way possible. Look at their face. Has it changed?

See, sense, or feel the person or symbol walking or fading away until they disappear. Take three deep breaths. Inhale through the nose and exhale through the mouth. Take three more deep breaths.

Nila F. Keith, C.H.T., who has been in private practice for more than thirty years, gave this process to us. She specializes in in-depth guidance of calling back your power and retrieving your fragmented soul parts.

Glossary

affirmation
A positive, repetitive declaration about something you want to manifest in your life. It always needs to be in the positive and present form.

altar
A table, stand, platform, etc. that holds sacred objects in dedication to the one creator/Spirit and a host of Gods and Goddesses.

amulet
A consecrated piece of jewelry or coin that is often worn or carried, which has been instilled with special desires.

anoint
To rub oil on something for ceremonial or magickal purposes.

astrology
The art-science of identifying and clarifying the basic personality traits of a person through reference to planetary movement and position.

athame
A ritual knife.

aura
The magnetic force field surrounding a human being, which can be seen or photographed as pulsating and floating colors. The colors reveal one's state of mind.

banish
To assertively drive energy away from a specific area or yourself.

Book of Shadows
Also known as a grimoire, a diary or journal of rituals, spells, and traditional lore.

chakra
Energy centers or vortexes located throughout body.

charge
To infuse an object with personal power.

cone of power
A method of directing the energy of an individual or group for a singular purpose or to provide a connection to Spirit.

consecrate
The act of cleansing and blessing an item, most often for magickal or spiritual purposes. May also include infusing or filling a focused intent into the item.

deosil
Clockwise, or going with the sun's direction. Used to gather, build, and strengthen positive energy.

divination
The art or practice of foretelling or predicting the future under the influence of Spirit.

dowsing rod
Usually made out of wood, this tool (shaped like an upside-down Y) is often used to find water as well as for divination.

dragon's blood
Bright red resin from a tropical plant and/or tree.

elements
The four fundamental substances (air, fire, water, and earth) that constitute physical matter.

energy
The celestial or primal force that is individually generated and can be combined with others for greater strength (as in a cone of power).

ether
The transient substance swirling throughout all spaces.

grounding
The act of centering or aligning oneself with the balance of nature and Spirit.

image candle
A candle infused with your unmatched energy, personality, and power.

incantation
A chant with the intention of bringing magick into your life.

infused oil
Herbs that have soaked in a carrier oil, such as olive, jojoba, or avocado oil for up to eight weeks.

intuition
To look in, consider, and respect the truth within yourself.

karma
The universal law and order of cause and effect, which demonstrates that whatever you do will come back to you.

magick
The relationship between focused will and Universal energy

meditation
An exercise requiring an emphasis on breathing and relaxing the mind's chatter for purposes of harmonizing and balancing oneself.

metaphysical
Events that occur beyond physical explanation.

Otherworld
The world where Spirits abide, waiting to be reborn.

paganism
Nature-based religion. The word *pagan* derives from the Latin word *paganus*, which means "peasant," and *pagus*, which translates to "country."

pantheon
Collection or group of Gods and Goddesses in a specific mythical or religious structure.

pentacle
A physical representation of a pentagram.

pentagram
A five-pointed star symbolizing the four elements in balance with Spirit.

rede
An advised plan of conduct and ethics.

reincarnation
The belief that life and death are a cycle. After you leave this life, you spend time with Spirit until you are reborn, to experience various situations and perspectives.

ritual
A sacred system of ceremonial acts in observance and of accordance with one's spirituality.

runes
An ancient alphabet inscribed on stones for the purpose of bringing in Spirit.

sabbat
One of eight festivals that celebrate earth, God, Goddess, and the ever-changing cycle of the seasons.

sacred space
A hallowed or blessed area that has been cleansed and prepared for magickal purposes.

smudging
A ritual to balance, protect, or purify yourself, others, a room, your crystals, or other special tools, using the smoke from an embering bundle of sage.

spell
To cast your word. A means of helping one channel or direct wishes and desires from the spiritual realm to the material.

Spirit
The ever-present life spark that exists as the Great Mystery, God, Goddess, Universe, and by many names, which exists in every being and living thing.

supernatural
Events and experiences occurring beyond the natural order of things. Also, unexplainable events and experiences attributed to the spiritual realm.

talisman
A consecrated item that brings good luck, averts evil, and embodies your personal magick.

tarot
Cards of archetypes, numbers, and symbols used to perceive the past, foretell the future, or divine current possible pathways.

thurible
An incense burner.

totem
An animal symbol or Spirit that guides one throughout life.

Underworld
The opposite side of the living under the rule of Hades, the Greek God of the dead.

visualization
The act of using your mind to "see" events outside your physically visual perception.

Wicca
A nature-based religion derived from the Anglo-Saxon root word *wicce*, meaning "to bend or shape" as well as "wise."

widdershins
Counterclockwise, or going against the sun's direction. Used to banish, wither, or remove unwanted energy.

zodiac
The visible path of the planets, sun, and moon around the earth; the twelve signs.

Recommended Reading

Adler, Margot. *Drawing Down the Moon: Witches, Druids, Goddess-Worshippers, and Other Pagans in America*. New York: Penguin, 2006.

Alexander, Skye. *The Modern Witchcraft Book of Tarot: Your Complete Guide to Understanding the Tarot*. New York: Adams Media, 2016.

Andrews, Ted. *Animal-Speak: The Spiritual & Magical Powers of Creatures Great & Small*. St. Paul, MN: Llewellyn Publications, 2002.

Aswynn, Freya. *Northern Mysteries and Magick: Runes & Feminine Powers*. St. Paul, MN: Llewellyn Publications, 2002.

Beyerl, Paul. *The Master Book of Herbalism*. Blaine, WA: Phoenix Publishing Inc., 1984

———. *A Compendium of Herbal Magic*. Blaine, WA: Phoenix Publishing Inc., 1998

Bonewits, Issac. *Bonewits's Essential Guide to Druidism*. New York: Citadel Press, 2006.

Buckland, Raymond. *Buckland's Complete Book of Witchcraft*. St. Paul, MN: Llewellyn Publications, 2002.

Budapest, Zsuzsanna E. *The Grandmother of Time: A Woman's Book of Celebrations, Spells, and Sacred Objects for Every Month of the Year*. New York: Harper One, 1989.

———. *The Holy Book of Women's Mysteries. Feminist Witchcraft, Goddess Rituals, Spellcasting, and Other Womanly Arts*. Berkeley, CA: Wingbow Press, 1989.

Campbell, Joseph. *Myths to Live By*. New York: Penguin, 1993.

Cunningham, Scott. *Cunningham's Encyclopedia of Magical Herbs*. St. Paul, MN: Llewellyn Publications, 1985.

———. *Wicca: A Guide for the Solitary Practitioner*. St. Paul, MN: Llewellyn Publications, 1988.

Forrest, Steven. *The Inner Sky: How to Make Wiser Choices for a More Fulfilling Life*. Borrego Springs, CA: Seven Paws Press, Inc., 2012.

Gawain, Shakti. *Creative Visualization: Use the Power of Your Imagination to Create What You Want in Your Life*. Novato, CA: New World Library, 2016.

Graves, Robert. *The White Goddess: A Historical Grammar of Poetic Myth*. New York: Farrar, Straus and Giroux, 2013.

Grimassi, Raven. *The Book of Holy Strega.* CreateSpace Independent Publishing Platform, 2012.

———. *Italian Witchcraft: The Old Religion of Southern Europe.* St. Paul, MN: Llewellyn Publications, 2000.

———. *Hereditary Witchcraft: Secrets of the Old Religion.* St. Paul, MN: Llewellyn Publications, 1999.

Hall, Judy. *The Crystal Bible.* Plano, TX: Walking Stick Press. 2003.

Harris, Eleanor L. *Ancient Egyptian Divination and Magic.* York Beach, ME: Samuel Weiser, Inc., 1998.

Hay, Louise. *You Can Heal Your Life.* Carlsbad, CA: Hay House, 1984.

Ingerman, Sandra. *Soul Retrieval: Mending the Fragmented Self.* New York: Harper One, 2006.

———. *Shamanic Journeying: A Beginner's Guide.* Boulder, CO: Sounds True, 2008.

———. *The Book of Ceremony: Shamanic Wisdom for Invoking the Sacred in Everyday Life.* Boulder, CO: Sounds True, 2018.

Judith, Anodea. *Wheels of Life: A User's Guide to the Chakra System.* St. Paul, MN: Llewellyn Publications, 1987.

Jung, Carl. *Man and His Symbols.* New York: Dell Publishing, 1964.

McCoy, Edain. *The Sabbats: A Witch's Approach to Living the Old Ways.* St. Paul, MN: Llewellyn Publications, 2002.

———. *A Witch's Guide to Faery Folk: How to Work with the Elemental World.* St. Paul, MN: Llewellyn Publications, 2002.

Moura, Ann. *Origins of Modern Witchcraft: The Evolution of a World Religion.* St. Paul, MN: Llewellyn Publications, 2000.

———. *Grimoire for the Green Witch: A Complete Book of Shadows.* Woodbury, MN: Llewellyn Publications, 2003.

Noble, Vicki. *Shakti Woman: Feeling Our Fire, Healing Our World.* San Francisco, CA: HarperSanFrancisco, 1991.

———. *The Double Goddess: Women Sharing Power.* Rochester, VT: Bear & Company, 2003.

Paxon, Diana L. *Taking Up The Runes: A Complete Guide To Using Runes In Spells, Rituals, Divination, And Magic.* York Beach, ME: Weiser Books, 2005.

———. *Odin: Ecstasy, Runes & Norse Magic.* Newburyport, MA: Weiser Books, 2017.

———. *Essential Asatru: Walking the Path of Norse Paganism.* New York: Citadel Press, 2006

Penczak, Christopher. *The Inner Temple of Witchcraft: Magick, Meditation, and Psychic Development.* St. Paul, MN: Llewellyn Publications, 2003.

Starhawk. *Spiral Dance: A Rebirth of the Ancient Religion of the Great Goddess.* San Francisco, CA: HarperSanFrancisco, 1999.

Toll, Maia and Kate O'Hara. *The Illustrated Herbiary: Guidance and Rituals from 36 Bewitching Botanicals.* North Adams, MA: Storey Publishing, 2016.

Weed, Susun. *Healing Wise.* Woodstock, NY: Ash Tree Publishing, 2003.

Wood, Matthew. *The Earthwise Herbal Repertory: The Definitive Practitioner's Guide.* Berkeley, CA: North Atlantic Books; 2016.

———.*The Earthwise Herbal, Volumes I & II: A Complete Guide to Old World Medicinal Plants.* Berkeley, CA: North Atlantic Books; 2008.

Weatherstone, Lunaea. *Tending Brigid's Flame: Awaken to the Celtic Goddess of Hearth, Temple, and Forge.* Woodbury, MN: Llewellyn Publications, 2015.

TAROT & ORACLE DECKS

Fairchild, Alana. *Kuan Yin Oracle: Blessings, Guidance & Enlightenment from the Divine Feminine.* St. Paul, MN: Llewellyn Publications, 2013.

Farmer, Steven. *Earth Magic Oracle Cards: A 48-Card Deck and Guidebook.* Carlsbad, CA: Hay House, 1994.

Greer, Bill F. *Morgan Greer Tarot Deck.* Stamford, CT: U.S. Games Systems, Inc., 2012.

Hall, Judy. *Crystal Wisdom Healing Oracle: 50 Oracle Cards for Healing, Self-Understanding, and Divination.* London, UK: Watkins Publishing, 2016.

Linn, Denise. *Sacred Traveler Oracle Cards: A 52-Card Deck and Guidebook.* Carlsbad, CA: Hay House, 2017.

Samms, Jamie and David Carson. *Medicine Cards: The Discovery of Power Through the Ways of Animals.* New York: St. Martin's Press, 1988.

Thompson, Siolo. *Hedgewitch Botanical Oracle.* St. Paul, MN: Llewellyn Publications, 2018.

Vogel, Karen and Vicki Noble. *The Motherpeace Round Tarot Deck: 78-Card Deck.* Stamford, CT: U.S. Games Systems, Inc., 2008.

Waitt, Arthur Edward. *The Rider Tarot Deck.* Stamford, CT: U.S. Games Systems, Inc., 1971.

Acknowledgments

There are many helping hands on the way to writing and publishing a book. The first of these is my glorious literary agent, Julie Castiglia, who carved out an author's path for me for which I am eternally grateful. In its original incarnation, this book was guided by Kirstie Melville, Windy Dorresteyn, and Lisa Regul.

Eighteen years later, this book has grown up and has been infused with the wisdom gained in those years. Thank you to my editor, Kimmy Tejasindhu, and designer, Sarah Rose Weitzman, for truly caring about the empowering message of this new revised book and helping bring that light-filled vision to life.

I am so thankful for the assistance of Yeshe Matthews, Raven Grimassi, Anna Korn, Lunaea Weatherstone, Jan Tjeerd, Brian Cain, and Rain Graves, who offered centuries of wisdom for the diverse paths of Witchcraft. And a great big shout out and thanks to all who gave spells and rituals, and all things magickal.

I am so appreciative of the continued inspiration of my children: Alethia, Skyler, and Kobe, who I think have come to appreciate having a Witch for a mama. And thank you to my love Joey Conti for always wanting the very best for me.

About the Author

JAMIE DELLA has studied magick and spirituality from around the world for more than twenty years. As a practitioner of healing arts, she leads workshops and ritual retreats on earth-based spirituality at the Northern California Women's Herbal Symposium. Jamie is the author of eight books, including *The Wicca Herbal* and *The Wicca Cookbook*, and writes the "Herbal Journeys" column in *Witches & Pagans* magazine. Several of her essays and articles have also been featured in online and print publications such as *Southwestern American Literary Journal*, *SageWoman* magazine, *Rebelle Society*, and the *Manifest-Station*.

Index

All rights reserved.
Published in the United States by Ten Speed Press, an imprint of Random House,
a division of Penguin Random House LLC, New York.
www.tenspeed.com

Ten Speed Press and the Ten Speed Press colophon are registered trademarks of
Penguin Random House LLC.

Originally published in paperback in slightly different form as *The Teen Spell
Book* in 2001.

Library of Congress Cataloging-in-Publication Data is on file with the publisher.

Hardcover ISBN: 978-1-9848-5702-6
eBook ISBN: 978-1-9848-5703-3

Printed in China

Design by Sarah Rose Weitzman

10 9 8 7 6 5 4

First Revised Edition